THE KEY ISSUES LECTURE SERIES
is made possible through a grant from
International Telephone and Telegraph Corporation

BUSINESS AND THE AMERICAN ECONOMY

1776-2001

Edited by
Jules Backman

With a Foreword by
Harold S. Geneen

New York: New York University Press   1976

78-2518

Preface

Abraham L. Gitlow

Dean, College of Business and
Public Administration
New York University

The Key Issues Lecture Series at the College of Business and Public Administration, New York University, is now represented by five volumes of these important lectures. This volume, the fifth in the series, collects the papers presented under the general topic *Business and the American Economy, 1776-2001*. The topic was selected because of its appropriateness in our nation's bicentennial year, a year in which it is especially suitable for us to take a glance back and to attempt to peer ahead.

The Key Issues Lecture Series has been made possible by a grant from the International Telephone and Telegraph Company. Its organizer and the editor of the published volumes is Professor Jules Backman, to whom all credit for the series is due. To both ITT and Professor Backman go the College's deep appreciation, for the series has enabled the College to enhance its role in advancing public understanding of many major contemporary issues.

The lecturers whose papers are included in this volume are a distinguished group, and we are completely confident that this volume will receive as excellent a reception as its predecessors have.

My personal appreciation goes also to Catherine Ferfoglia, Professor Backman's secretary and principal aide in preparing the volume for publication, and to my administrative assistants, Susan Greenbaum and Virginia Moress.

Contents

Foreword

Harold S. Geneen

Chairman and Chief Executive

International Telephone and Telegraph Corporation

With the founding of the American commonwealth, a revolution in men's expectations and behavior became possible. The colonists rebelled partly out of anger at British businessmen trying to insure themselves a monopoly on selling goods on our shores, preventing local manufacture.

So, from the beginning, commerce became synonymous with America and freedom. But can that cherished spirit of personal effort, commerce and adventure—that "Yankee pride" which spawned two centuries of self-confidence—now long endure?

Let us realize that ahead lies the addition of another 200 million people in the United States, doubling the density of our country in just 40 to 50 years hence. What adjustments must business make to meet this economic challenge? Can any of us fathom the pressures this population strain will bring to the free enterprise system?

We, at ITT, believe firmly that an accurate understanding of the events and impulses that helped achieve the overwhelming supremacy of the U.S. economy is essential to finding meaning for

American life ahead. This book re-examines the American Experience and identifies trends that threaten the free enterprise system, a system that could be called the "freedom of choice" system because its purpose—in fact, its only means of surviving—is to be highly attentive to our personal freedoms of choice.

I continue to believe the university campus is one of the most important focal points where the free enterprise system *must* take its stand. Institutions of the calibre of NYU can and do lend their support to the continuance of many of our important values—and do so within the lasting disciplines of economic reality.

That's why we were grateful to sponsor this special Bicentennial edition of the Key Issues Lecture Series at NYU's College of Business and Public Administration.

In the period ahead, American business will recruit its future executives from the ranks of those graduates having rising expectations. I'm confident it will be a formidable group of candidates.

ONE

Past Growth and Future Prospects *

Jules Backman

Research Professor Emeritus of Economics
New York University

THE FIRST 200 YEARS

The structure of the American economy has changed dramatically during the past 200 years. At the beginning of the period we were largely an agricultural economy and relied heavily on imports for most manufactured products. We were as Roger Blough states "a seriously underdeveloped nation." Throughout the nineteenth century and up to World War II, our relative dependence upon agriculture declined and mining and manufacturing became increasingly important. After World War II, the relative importance of mining and manufacturing declined, while the service industries grew steadily more important. The broad trends are summarized in a few key figures:

Employment in agriculture declined from 95 percent of the total in 1776 to 50 percent in 1876 and only 4 percent in 1975.
The relative importance of employment in manufacturing and

* My special thanks to Marvin Levine, who provided valuable assistance in the collection of materials for this chapter.

mining was 20 percent in 1876, reached a peak of 44 percent in
World War II and then declined to about 25 percent in 1975.

The so-called *service* producing industries (these include transportation and public utilities, wholesale and retail trade, finance, insurance, and real estate, services, and government) have accounted for a
significant increase in the percent of employees on nonagricultural
payrolls:

1919	52.7 percent
1929	57.6
1947	57.9
1957	60.4
1974	68.5
1975	70.7

The increase in the service sphere was marked particularly in
government employment which rose from 9.9 percent in 1919 to 18.1
percent in 1975.[1] In contrast, the decline in the goods-producing
sector is particularly noted in mining. This shift in the composition of
employment reflects the changing pattern of demand in an affluent
society. As an economy expands, there is a relative shift of demand
from food and clothing to a broad range of industrial goods and to
the enjoyment of various services.

The shift of labor out of agriculture and into manufacturing
increased significantly the overall productivity of our economy, since
manufacturing in the nineteenth and early twentieth centuries was
the most technologically advanced sector. Facilitating this development, as Roger Blough points out, were "the freedom of group
organization, and the freedom of interplay between the groups and
the freedom of initiative within a group." The most important of
these groups was the corporation.

Growth of the American Economy

In two centuries, then, we have grown from a small agricultural country to an industrial giant. We were fortunate to have diversified mineral resources, rich agricultural land, ample supplies of water, good climate, and a people strongly endowed with a work ethic. We had a free-enterprise system which encouraged individuals to work hard since they could reap the fruits of their efforts, two oceans protected us from external aggression, and on our northern and southern borders we had friendly countries with relatively sparse populations. Thus, we were not threatened by invasions such as those that periodically devastated so many parts of Europe.

This was truly a land of opportunity and was so regarded throughout the world. As a result, our population was swelled by a flow of immigrants who brought diversified talents to this country and provided the manpower required to develop it.

We were the beneficiaries in the first half of the nineteenth century of patterns of producing manufactured goods that contained the basic elements of modern mass production. This entailed the manufacture of standardized products that were characterized by interchangeable parts and the use of a growing number of machine tools and specialized items, together with abundant power. Thus, we substituted simplified and mechanical operations for the approach of the craftsman. At the same time, there were significant developments in the organization of productive effort and in the methods of marketing standardized quantity products. By the midnineteenth century these features had been successfully applied in a number of industries.

Roger Blough finds as "extraordinary the contribution over the years of the improvements in group activity techniques, or if you please, in management." These developments met far less resistance in the United States than in other countries. Actually, the new approaches were facilitated by the existing social framework and were accepted and encouraged.

The economy of the United States was being industrialized before the Civil War. The war stimulated this development. In the second half of the nineteenth century, industrialization was encouraged by the growth of railroads that helped to create a national market. This ever-expanding network hastened the growth of existing commercial centers such as New York and Philadelphia, as well as the growth of cities such as Chicago and Atlanta. The expansion of railroads increased the demand for consumer goods and developed the first large market for producers goods.

Adequate data are not available to allow us to make a precise measurement of all aspects of economic growth for the 200-year period. Population increased from 3.9 million in 1790 to 214 million in 1975. In 1790, about 95 percent of the population was classified as rural with relatively low productivity.[2] Professor Solomon Fabricant estimates that "Total product . . . multiplied 1500 times over the 200-year period" (see Chapter 2).

Rough data are available showing the general magnitude of changes in real gross national product and in industrial production for the past century:

Real gross national product increased by 1550 percent or an average of 4.4 percent per year between 1869-1873 and 1929.[3] Between 1929 and 1974, the increase was 400 percent or an annual average of 3.2 percent.[4]

Manufacturing production increased by 1373 percent or an average of 4.1 percent between 1869 and 1929.[5] Between 1929 and 1974, the increase was 546 percent or an annual average of 3.8 percent.[6]

We have expanded our economy at a compound rate of 3 to 4 percent over the past century. While these appear to be modest rates of increase, they mean that we have been able to double our real output every 18 to 24 years.

Of course, this growth has been uneven. Cyclical forces have been reflected in periods of recession and depression of various depths and durations. In this connection, the depressions of 1873, 1893, 1907, 1921 and the long depression of the 1930s were among the most important. During periods of expansion, growth has been more rapid than the 3 to 4 percent long-term rate in order to overcome the declines which developed during recessions and depressions. But despite these interruptions, the latest of which was the 1973-1975 recession, our economy has continued to move upward to new high ground.

Levels of living have risen to among the highest in the world. While, by our standards, there remain important pockets of poverty, there has been a general sharing of the fruits of this growth. In the United States, the composition of those at the lowest rung of the ladder has changed significantly—largely immigrants with high hopes many years ago to those whose social situation makes it so difficult to break out into broader society. For example, the teenage unemployment rate for blacks in 1974 in poverty areas was 36.1 percent and in nonpoverty areas 29.5 percent.[7]

Real incomes have risen significantly during the present century. The rise in hourly earnings made it possible to achieve satisfactory levels of living by working fewer hours so that real weekly earnings have continued to rise despite the decline in the number of hours worked a week—from about 60 at the turn of the century to an average of under 40 today. But this rise in incomes also had important social effects. With the head of the family able to earn an income adequate to maintain his family, child labor, which was very important in the nineteenth century, has been virtually eliminated. The long hours of work and low pay for children had significant adverse social and economic effects. With the education laws of many of the states requiring matriculation in school until age 16 or older, much has been done to insure a better quality of the work force. Moreover, the increase in educational opportunity has been a significant factor in our rising level of productivity.

An increasing number of women has entered the labor force in recent decades. The participation rate for women in the mid-1950s to mid-1960s was concentrated in the age group from 45 to 64. In the last decade, the most substantial increase was for younger women from 20 to 34. Those entering the labor force have more education with a higher proportion having some college training.[8]

The Role of Energy

A vital contribution to the past growth of our economy was an ample supply of low-cost energy.[9] In our earliest days, this energy first was provided by wood and then substantially by coal. These fuels powered the steam engine and also were used directly. Even after electric power was discovered, it was generated from coal and became a prime source of energy. In time, fuel oil and natural gas became the main sources of electric power.[10] Petroleum also has provided the energy for our extensive transportation system, built around the internal combustion engine, and for home and factory heating. Since World War II there has also been a slow development of nuclear energy.

In the past two decades, it became increasingly clear that energy supplies of petroleum and natural gas would become more limited and more expensive. To a greater extent we were relying heavily on foreign sources for crude petroleum and refined products. In 1960, imports of crude oil and petroleum products accounted for 15 percent of domestic consumption, by 1965 imports were 21 percent, and in 1974 they were 37 percent.[11] The Arab oil boycott late in 1973 brought this point home to the major industrial countries.[12] Sharply higher prices for gasoline, fuel oil, and other petroleum products were experienced by business and consumers throughout the world and contributed to the combination of price inflation and recession widely experienced in the 1973-1975 period. As a result, as we approached our bicentennial year, the era of cheap energy ended and a new period of higher-cost energy began. This development will lead to lower rates of economic growth as resources are diverted to the development of greater supplies of energy domestically.[13]

Organizational Structure

The organizational structure of business also has changed significantly, as Roger Blough spells out (see Chapter 4). In our early history, the individual proprietorship and partnership predominated. In a small-scale economy, modest sums of money were involved in business operations and unlimited liability posed no overwhelming challenge. Early in the nineteenth century the need to raise substantial sums of capital set the stage for the corporate form which offered the advantage of limited liability to investors.

By 1939, corporations accounted for 77.3 percent of business receipts, although they accounted for only 26.2 percent of the number of concerns. By 1972, the relative number of corporations had declined to 14.0 percent but the volume of business accounted for had increased to 85.1 percent.[14]

During the past two decades, the multinational corporation has become increasingly important as companies began to operate on a worldwide scale. This is true not only of companies based in the United States but for those based in Japan, England, West Germany, France, Holland, and other industrial countries.[15] The urge for expansion has driven firms, from early times, to develop markets overseas. Most of the largest corporations now operate on a world-wide scale with some obtaining one-third to one-half of their volume abroad. This includes such companies in the *Fortune* 500 as Burroughs, Exxon, Heinz, International Telephone and Telegraph, United Shoe Machinery, Colgate-Palmolive, Anaconda, Singer, Mobil, Pfizer, Otis, National Cash Register, Sterling Drug, Warner-Lambert, Standard Oil of California, and Texaco.[16] Professor Schiff notes that the internationalization of business creates problems because of differences in accounting standards among countries.

Big business now accounts for a major part of manufacturing, mining, and public utilities. Small business is found mainly in retail and wholesale trade, construction, services, agriculture, finance, and real estate. Although the relative importance of receipts accounted for by unincorporated business has been declining, the total number of such firms has continued to increase substantially.[17]

Role of Technology

Economic growth has been significantly affected by the dramatic changes in technology which have characterized our history. The developments in transportation and communications facilitated the opening of a continent. Electric power provided a new dimension for energy. The automobile resulted in enormous demands for materials, provided many jobs, and affected significantly our life style. The computer set the stage for the era of automation. John Diebold concludes that "information technology is entering the take-off phase." Roger Blough attributes our progress in these areas to "a truly amazing aggregation of individuals in the business world" whose activities were complemented by expanded "group activity."

New technology has set the pace for the development of many industries of which the organic chemicals, data processing, and electronics are recent illustrations. Technology has reduced the required labor input dramatically for many industries with the accompanying increase in output per manhour which in turn has been a key factor in our rising levels of living. Thus, new inventions, innovations, growth of knowledge in the form of research and development, changes in techniques of management, and other activities have enhanced technology in our society.[18] The continual search for new products and processes has played a crucial role in the economic development of the United States.

The Role of Money and Banking

We have moved from an economy which used mainly currency to one in which checks account for about 90 percent of the dollar value of all transactions. With the development of the computer, the stage is now being set for the next quantum jump in this area, namely, the checkless society.[19] We have already reached an intermediate stage in which we use credit cards, with the result that payments are made for a variety of transactions with a single check. John Diebold foresees "A banking system integrating customers of all kinds into one total management system."

The banking system provides a free flow of credit throughout the country through the clearing operations of the Federal Reserve System. However, we still place constraints upon the ability of a bank to have offices in more than one state, although banks are permitted to establish branches overseas. The nature and number of future branches may be changed dramatically by the computer. According to John Diebold, "Introduction of a data terminal directly linked to the central information system of a bank has made virtually any location a potential branch bank—a supermarket, a store front, even a telephone booth."

As our economy has expanded, the banks have provided the credit resources required to facilitate the smooth flow of commerce. Prior to

1933, when the banking system broke down, widespread bank failures characterized our history. For example, in the panic of 1907 a large number of banks failed. This development helped to bring about the creation of the Federal Reserve System in 1913 but it didn't stop bank failures.

Since the debacle of the 1930s, failures have been fewer and depositors have been given protection through the Federal Deposit Insurance Corporation which guarantees bank deposits up to a stipulated maximum - currently $40,000. Moreover, as Dr. Andrew Brimmer's analysis shows, the Federal Reserve System stands ready to move in where a major bank is in difficulty in order to prevent the adverse impact on the economy of such a failure. Thus, the Federal Reserve closely monitored the growing problems at Franklin National—a severe liquidity crisis, difficulty in raising short-term funds, and heavy foreign-exchange losses. The Federal Reserve System moved to resolve the difficulties, and ultimately Franklin National was acquired by a sound banking institution (see Chapter 5).[20]

Role of Accounting

As the American economy has expanded and corporations have grown in relative size and in complexity, the need for more sophisticated record keeping has become increasingly important. Moreover, as the tasks performed by the computer have increased in scope, the need for accurate business information to feed into computers also has become greater. At the same time, the ability to use and misuse accounting records has grown considerably (for example, Equity Funding), posing new problems for the accountant.

The latest developments in this long evolution have been accelerated by a major merger movement, sharp increases in the number of conglomerates, the growth of the multinational firm, and the persistent peacetime price inflation throughout the world. As Professor Michael Schiff notes, these developments have provided new challenges to the accounting profession. From the simple record keeping required in an agrarian economy and in the early stages of industrialization, we have evolved into an era of very sophisticated accounting records. With the widespread ownership of corporate securities, there also has developed greater emphasis upon the need for public disclosure of a corporation's activities—an important battleground in the 1970s.

The Quality of Life

Up to the past decade, we were concerned primarily with the level of living. Improvements in medical care, more diversified diets, and other developments have added to the quality of life. But such progress was incidental to our efforts to raise our levels of living. However, attention is now being directed increasingly to the quality of life. Policies have been adopted to reduce air and water pollution. The health hazards involved in some drugs and food products are being more extensively evaluated. Better health care is being made available to the elderly and to lower-income groups. The quality and hazards of urban living have caused increasing concern—although progress in overcoming urban problems still is slow.

To improve the quality of life involves costs, and hence some sacrifice must be made in the rate of growth in our level of living. Our available resources probably will not permit both an improvement in the quality of life and the continuation of past rates of growth in the levels of living. However, as our levels of living have attained ever higher peaks, it has become possible to forgo some increases in order to improve the quality of life.[21] The extent to which this trade off should take place is one of the important decisions to be made as we reach our bicentennial year.[22]

Equal Opportunity and Education

There also has been increasing concern over the economic status of minority groups, particularly, the blacks, Puerto Ricans, and Mexican Americans. The Supreme Court decision in 1954 ruled that separate schools for blacks and whites resulted in unequal education and the Civil Rights Act of 1964 substantially speeded up enforcement of that decision.[23] As a result, considerable progress has been made in equalizing educational opportunities, a necessary first step in achieving economic equality. Federal and state laws have required equal opportunities for minority groups. One result has been more job opportunities for minorities. Progress inevitably has been slow but progress has been made.

Discrimination by sex always has been characteristic of our society. In the past decade or so both government and the private sector have moved to eradicate such discrimination. Thus, the Equal Pay Act of 1963, requires employers to pay men and women in the same plant the same wage for work of equivalent skill and responsibility, the Civil Rights Act of 1964 prohibits discrimination in such aspects of employment as hiring and firing, and the Equal Employment Opportunity Act of 1972 gives the government enforcement power in the courts.

Educational opportunities have been broadened considerably. An ever-increasing number of high school graduates have gone to college. Open admissions made possible college education for many members of lower income and underprivileged groups.

The widespread extension of education is shown in the accompanying table.

	Number of High School Graduates	Number of College Graduates
	(thousands)	
1870	16	9
1900	95	27
1920	311	49
1940	1221	187
1960	1351	392
1970	2896	827
1975 (est.)	3119	1029
1980 (est.)	3043	1091

In the few colleges we had in the eighteenth century the main emphasis was upon preparation for the ministry and to some extent for teaching. Now, we prepare students for all types of roles in life through institutions for such professions as law, dentistry, medicine, and engineering and offer a wide variety of higher education institutions ranging from two-year colleges to a full range of graduate programs.

Expanding Role of the Federal Government

The Federal Government may affect the economy through its expenditures and taxes and by its regulation of economic activity. On both bases, it played a relatively minor role in our early history. At the end of the nineteenth century, Federal Government receipts and expenditures were equal to slightly more than 3 percent of the national income; almost three-fourths of the expenditures were for the armed forces, veterans compensation, and interest on the public debt.[25]

Carl Kaysen divides the first 200 years into four periods (see Chapter 3). The first period covers our first century when government actions directly affecting business were concerned mainly with such matters as tariffs.

The second period (1880-1930) "saw an outburst of growth in Federal regulation of markets. The bases of the regulatory framework under which we currently operate was created at this time." The Interstate Commerce Act (1887) to regulate railroads, the Sherman Antitrust Act (1890) to regulate monopoly and encourage competition, and the Pure Food and Drug Act (1906) were among the early efforts undertaken to regulate business activities in our second century.

Prior to the Great Depression of the 1930s, the Federal Government played a minor role in our economy. Total Federal spending in 1929 was still only about 3 percent of national income. However, this situation changed dramatically between 1930 and 1945, the third period identified by Dr. Kaysen. By 1939, Federal spending had reached 12.3 percent of national income as we sought to "spend our way" out of the Great Depression through deficit financing. A host of laws were enacted extending Federal regulation to labor, agriculture, public utilities, securities markets, and other sectors of the economy.

The fourth period covers 1945 to 1975. The post-World War II period witnessed a further extension of the role of the Federal Government. The Employment Act of 1946 established the goal of maintaining a high level of employment and increasing emphasis was given to attempts to regulate the level of economic activity, especially through fiscal policy. Social security was liberalized to raise benefits and to provide medicare for the elderly. Environmental goals were established, equal opportuntiy legislation was passed, tougher standards were set to determine the legality of mergers, price and wage controls were introduced, and periodically government intervened in private pricing decisions, programs were adopted in the areas of education and health care and to help small business, the consumer, and the unemployed, and regulation was imposed on international investment. Largely because of these programs, Federal Government spending had increased to about one-quarter of the national income as we approached the bicentennial year.

Clearly, we have come a long way from the laissez faire environment that prevailed prior to the 1930s. Although economic activity still is carried on overwhelmingly in the private sector, to an increasing degree the Federal Government has been setting the rules of the game.

THE NEXT TWENTY-FIVE YEARS

Attempts to forecast the future are fraught with considerable risk and usually have proven to be wide of the mark. The dangers inherent in forecasting where we will be in 25 years are well illustrated if we turn the clock back to 1950. Could we foresee in that year many of the dramatic events and trends which have taken place: the record peacetime inflation of the 1970s, the sharp decline in the birth rate, the enormous rise in the price of gold, the shift of the dollar from the strongest currency in the world to a weak one, the historically high level of interest rates, the development of the Euro-dollar market, the dramatic growth of the computer industry, the development of miracle drugs, the resignations of a president and vice president of the United States, the growing emphasis on the quality of life, the concern over job opportunities for minority groups, the space program and landing a man on the moon, 85 million persons employed, the Arab oil boycott and the accompanying problems, a 131 percent increase in real GNP, Federal budgets in excess of $350 billion, the rapid growth of Japan and West Germany, and many other developments?

Wars, new inventions, changes in tastes and habits, social changes, and other forces—many unforeseen—have upset the most carefully prepared forecasts. Many economic projections in the past have erred on the side of pessimism, although we have had our periods of overoptimism (for example, during the 1920s and the 1960s). Currently, concern over exhaustion of supplies of raw materials has produced a new crop of Cassandras. However, to this observer it appears that we will continue to experience economic growth, but that the pattern of the American economy for the balance of the twentieth century will be influenced most significantly by a number of recent developments, particularly those during the past decade, and by the policy options we adopt in the next few years.

The Quality of Life

There has emerged in recent years a consensus that new pollution must be stopped or considerably abated and that efforts must be made to eliminate past environmental pollution. A major manifestation of this national resolve was the creation of the Environmental Protection Agency (EPA) in 1969 to develop quality standards for air and water. Specific actions have included the establishment of standards to reduce pollutants by the automobile, the restrictions on the use of high sulfur coal and oil in the production of electric power, and the elimination of efflusions into our streams by the chemical, paper, and other industries.[26]

To accomplish these objectives, it has been necessary for private industry to modify the polluting effects of existing plants and to increase its investment in new plants.[27] In 1975, business planned to spend $6.3 billion on pollution abatement (in 1973 it was $4.9 billion, and in 1974 it was $5.6 billion). Such spending is about 5 per cent of total new plant and equipment expenditures.[28]

What will be the total cost of cleaning up the environment? No one really knows. Officially, it has been estimated it would cost $25 to $30 billion annually for at least a decade. Meyer and Ingram have suggested that: "$10 to $20 billion of annual outlays is not a fully unrealistic estimate of what might be required to clean up auto emissions alone." [29] The electric utilities have found it very difficult to finance both pollution control and the required expansion in capacity. This could involve an unmeasurable cost in terms of future brownouts and blackouts. With the total supply of savings limited, the billions of dollars required to eliminate pollution will mean a smaller volume of resources available to finance an expansion of capacity. As a result there will be a slower rate of growth in our average level of living. Per capita real income increased at an annual rate of 2.2 percent between 1929 and 1974.[30] A fractionally lower rate of increase is probable during the balance of the twentieth century. This is a desirable trade off.

The Energy Problem

We have moved into a new era of high-cost energy with serious uncertainty as to reliability of the flow of supplies. Our heavy dependence upon imported petroleum puts us at the mercy of the OPEC.[31] The development of alternative sources of energy—nuclear, solar, oil shale, off-shore drilling, gasification—would take up to a decade or more even under the most favorable circumstances. But the required changes in public policy have not been made, as Congress has been reluctant to make hard and unpopular decisions.[32] Moreover, there has been a great reluctance to initiate the required measures of conservation in order to reduce our dependence on overseas sources of supply. Valuable time has been lost. One result will be a somewhat slower rate of economic growth in the years ahead.

The prospective shortage of petroleum portends changes in the American life style which has been built around the widespread use of the automobile. Higher costs for gasoline and limited supplies will tend to hold down the rate of growth in automobile use, should lead to greater demand for smaller cars or much more efficient use of gasoline in larger cars, could reduce the movement to suburbia and exurbia, will affect the types of vacations we take, and should lead to greater investment in mass-transportation facilities. To the extent that conservation is affected by higher prices, consumers will be faced with the choice of cutting their effective demand for petroleum products or reducing their consumption of other goods and services.

Slower Rate of Population Growth

Although the population explosion is still a worldwide problem, this is not true in the United States where we face a slowdown in population growth. Changing life styles and the pill combined to reduce the birth rate from 25.3 per 1000 in 1957 to 15.0 in 1973. The change in the role of women has been significant: there has been a greater number of females working, they have achieved higher levels of education, and they have become more economically independent.

Because of the decline in the birth rate, the Bureau of the Census projects the median estimate of population for the year 2000 at 262 million. This would be an annual rate of growth of only 0.8 percent; in the preceding quarter of a century, 1949 to 1974, total population increased at an annual rate of 1.4 percent. Moreover, the actual increase in the next 25 years is estimated at 50 million persons or less than the increase of 63 million in the last 25 years.[33] Interestingly, in 1974, for the first time, the average household in this country dropped below three persons.[34]

A slower rate of population growth will act to restrain the growth in gross national product and in consumption and, in time, will limit the rate of increase in the labor force.[35] It has already reduced the pressure for expansion by public schools and universities. These developments could shave a little off the annual rate of growth to which we have been accustomed in the past.

In connection with such population projections, it must be kept in mind that they may be modified in relatively short periods of time and the change may affect significantly the related estimates of labor force and real GNP. For example, based on total population of 194.6 million in 1965, Kahn and Wiener projected a total population at 222 million for 1975 and 318.4 million for the year 2000; this was an increase of 1.5 percent per year.[36] Population actually reached only 214 million in 1975 and is now projected at 262 million for 2000. This is a shortfall of about 18 percent and affects significantly their projections of GNP for the end of the century.

Greater Proportion of Older Persons

The mix of the population has been changing so that a steadily larger proportion is 65 years and older; the proportion has increased from 8.1 percent in 1950 to 10.5 percent in 1975. On the basis of projected trends of total population, the proportion of older citizens is estimated to continue to rise, reaching about 12 percent in 2000.[37]

The increases in benefits and coverage under social security and private pensions have permitted older workers to retire at an earlier age and with more income. Between 1960 and 1974 the labor force participation rate for males 65 and over fell from 33.1 to 22.4 percent.[38] For 1990, the proportion is projected at 19.3 percent.[39]

During the 1973-1975 recession, early retirements, that is before 65 years of age, were encouraged by many businesses and government agencies.[40] To the extent that unemployment continues to be a persistent problem, this trend could continue. Three results flow from this development: (1) a smaller proportion of the population will be working and will have to support those who are retired, (2) experienced workers will be lost to the economy, and (3) there will be an increasing burden on the Social Security System.

Growing Importance of Services

The evolution of the American economy into a service economy is bound to have an adverse effect on long-term rates of increase in output per manhour.[41] Historically, the rate of increase in OPM was significantly influenced by the above-average rates of increase in mining, transportation and communications, and public utilities where the large-scale application of capital made a significant contribution to productivity. Many of the service industries, such as barbershops, operate on a one-to-one basis, and hence large-scale use of capital could not play a major role. As a result, the gains in OPM in those areas have been nominal. A slower rate of growth in OPM will act to hold down the rate of increase in real per capita income and thus in the levels of living.[42]

Equality of Employment Opportunities

Discrimination in employment on the basis of religion, race, color, and sex has been familiar throughout our history. In recent years, there has been a strong drive to reduce such discrimination. Legislation has played a significant role and the affected groups have had powerful voices raised in their behalf. Some of the barriers to religious discrimination began to fall first. Now the major emphasis is on the other types.

Building upon the base established in the last decade, we should witness the elimination of wage differentials between men and women for the same job. Job opportunities for members of minority groups should continue to expand—at all levels. The breaking down of job barriers will encourage members of minority groups to pursue their education more assiduously and thus reduce the number of school dropouts. The higher level of education in turn will qualify them for more responsible jobs. The economy will benefit because of the better trained labor force.

While it is utopian to expect all discrimination to end, we should make substantial progress toward that goal before we enter the twenty-first century. It will be necessary to maintain a high level of economic activity to assure equal employment opportunity for all. During slack periods, minorities suffer significantly due to lack of education, seniority arrangements in union contracts, and related factors. On balance, the reduction in discrimination will add skilled workers to the labor force and thus provide a partial offset to the negative factors discussed earlier.

Shortages of Raw Materials and Capital

The worldwide boom which culminated in 1973 was characterized by growing shortages of many basic materials. The results were production bottlenecks which held down total output and sharply higher prices which acted to ration the limited supplies to their most urgent uses. In this country, many of the shortages of basic materials reflected not only the worldwide pressures but in large part the earlier failure to expand capacity because of low profit margins in some industries, the price-control program, and the high cost of cleaning up and preventing pollution which diverted investment funds otherwise available to expand capacity.

Some recent analysts, particularly the MIT-Club of Rome, have emphasized that the lack of availability of basic raw materials will act as a barrier to growth in the twenty-first century; they have recommended policies to hold down the growth rate in order to stretch out the available supplies of these materials.

Thus, the much-criticized Club of Rome Report noted:

> Given present resource consumption rates and the projected increase in these rates, the great majority of the currently important nonrenewable resources will be extremely costly 100 years from now. The above statement remains true regardless of the most optimistic assumptions about undiscovered reserves, technological advances, substitution, or recycling, as long as the demand for resources continues to grow exponentially.[43]

Two conclusions of the Club of Rome study were that:

> 1. If the present growth trends in world population, industrialization, pollution, food production, and resource depletion continue unchanged, the limits to growth on this planet will be reached sometime within the next one hundred years.
> 2. It is possible to alter these growth trends and to establish a condition of ecological and economic stability that is sustainable far into the future.[44]

In connection with such forecasts as that of the Club of Rome, however, it must be recalled that dramatic changes in technology have made possible large increases in available supplies of raw materials in the past, despite forebodings concerning their future adequacy.

Professor Fabricant is more optimistic than the Club of Rome: "What we now count as resources are but a tiny fraction of the mass of our earth. In fact, resources as defined in a valid economic sense, and the economic yield from resources, have also been increasing. . . . I see no good reason to fear a decline in the foreseeable future in the rate of growth of resources and of the income or output they yield, to a level below or even only down to the rate of population growth."

There is growing agreement that enormous amounts of capital investment will be needed to modernize American plant and equipment and to finance the expansion in capacity required to enable us to continue on the path of economic growth in the future.[45]

To raise the required amounts of new capital will require the inducement of satisfactory profit rates and appropriate tax incentives. It is a vital prerequisite to obtaining the economic growth which is essential to permit us to meet our large list of social and economic needs. This growth must be induced and nurtured by assuring a proper economic environment.

The Role of Government

The regulation of industry by government has expanded enormously in the past two decades.[46] A key question is the extent to which regulation will be increased in the future. Roger M. Blough notes "the undesirable effects on production of the intertwining vines of regulation" and concludes that: "The payload for the nation from group activity in the field of production during the coming decades will depend on the flexibility given it. That flexibility, that decentralized decision making is the bread of life in the functioning of business units."

In our complex economy, decisions are made by a myriad of businesses which must have freedom to carry out those decisions within a broad framework of government regulatory policies. The more detailed those regulations, the less flexibility there will be in taking the new initiatives required for an expanding economy. The heavy hand of regulation on the railroads already has taken its toll. The flow of new life-giving drugs has been slowed up in a web of regulations. The development of nuclear energy—so vital to freeing us from heavy dependence upon the oil exporting states (OPEC)—has been delayed.

As we seek to improve the quality of life, we must heed these lessons of the past and rely more upon the carrot than on the stick. A continuation of the trends toward more intensive regulation as in recent years can act to inhibit economic growth rates.

The Size of the Economy in 2001

Professor Solomon Fabricant concludes "We may expect that national product and product per capita will continue to grow." However, he offers no numerical projections because "no one can predict with precision what the rate of economic growth will be." Past "experience suggests that the value of [such projections] is limited."

There can be no quarreling with his conclusion. Nevertheless, forward planning requires some projections of anticipated broad trends. One way to meet this problem is to present a range of projections rather than a single number. Keeping in mind Professor Fabricant's warning, the following ranges of projections are offered.

What will be the size of our economy in the year 2001? In 1974, real gross national product (GNP) in 1958 dollars was $821 billion. If the economy grows at the rate of 3.5 percent compounded annually, the total would be $2079 billion in the year 2001; a 4 percent growth rate would yield $2368 billion.

However, because of some fundamental changes, including a lower rate of population growth and the resulting smaller prospective increases in the labor force, the energy problem, and the increasing importance of services, a lower growth rate is a strong probability.[47] If the growth rate is 3 percent, total real GNP would increase to $1824 billion or a little more than double the 1974 total. On the basis of assumed growth rates of 3 to 4 percent, real GNP in the year 2001 would be between $1824 billion and $2368 billion in 1958 dollars. It should be noted that fractional changes in the projected annual growth rate cumulate into significant aggregate differences over a period of 27 years.

The actual rate of growth undoubtedly will vary from the above projections. But one thing is fairly certain. As Professor Fabricant concludes: "... we may expect that the composition of final output will change as new goods and services displace old, as relative prices are altered, as incomes rise and tastes change, and government regulations affecting the production of individual commodities are imposed or modified or repealed."

Real per capita disposable personal income (DPI) was $4623 in 1974. In the past, real per capita DPI has increased at an annual rate of 2.3 percent. If the future repeats the past, the average would be $8542 in the year 2001. However, a lower rate of increase is probable in the future as resources are diverted to improve the quality of life and as we become increasingly a service economy. At a compound rate of increase of 1.5 percent, the total would be $6910 and at 2.0 percent, it would be $7891. For a family of three, the total was $13,869 and for a family of four it was $18,492 in 1974. The projected trends are as follows:

	Projected Per Capita Disposable Personal Income, 2001	
	(in 1974 dollars)	
Annual Rate of Increase	Family of Three	Family of Four
1.5%	$20,730	$27,640
2.0	23,673	31,564
2.3	25,626	34,168

With an increasing proportion of the population consisting of elderly persons, a higher divorce rate, later marriages, and a declining birth rate, an average family of about three is the more likely prospect for the year 2001. Even at the lowest rate of increase, the average family of three would have achieved an overall increase of about 50 percent in its level of living by the beginning of the next century. This projection assumes no change in income tax rates—an unlikely prospect. Higher tax rates would reduce the rate of increase and vice versa.

The projection also assumes that real growth rates will be held down because of diversion of resources to improve the quality of life. Thus, the real improvement in economic *and* personal well-being will be greater than suggested by the projections noted above.

The Business Cycle Is Not Dead

In the early 1960s, there was widespread celebration over the "death of the business cycle." The chief celebrants were a number of economists who thought they had discovered methods to "fine tune" the economy and thus to minimize or to avoid future recessions or depressions. At the worst, they were ready to concede that there would be periods of slower growth—rather than actual declines—in economic activity. A new phrase, "growth recession," was coined to describe this situation.

The events of the past decade—and particularly of the 1970s— showed clearly that the reports of the business cycle's death were premature. On the basis of the available evidence there is every reason to believe that we will continue to have periodic downturns in business activity during the remainder of this century. As Professor Fabricant concludes: "The rates of growth will not be steady; they will vary from one year to another, and sometimes become negative, for the business cycle has been moderated but not eliminated."

The art of politics assures an unwillingness by government to impose the restrictive measures required to prevent a boom from getting out of hand. And the willingness to underwrite expansionary fiscal measures and to insist upon liberal monetary policies assure that it will. These policies are designed to maintain maximum employment and thus to limit unemployment. Unfortunately, they usually result in excessive rates of price inflation which set the stage for an even larger amount of unemployment as was so clearly demonstrated in 1974-1975.

In the business community, excessive accumulations of inventories as a protection against anticipated shortages or as a hedge against projected price inflation will continue to require periods of liquidation. Excessive expansion of plant capacity will be followed by catch-up periods in which to utilize the capacity and an accompanying cutback in new investment. The inflationary policies of governments will continue to create distortions in the economy and the need to provide "cooling off" periods to correct them.

The magnitude of recessions and depressions should be more moderate than in the pre-World War II period. But moderation does not mean elimination. It must be recognized that the so-called built-in stabilizers—unemployment compensation, declining income tax collections which lead to Federal budgetary deficits, and other income stabilizing policies—must be triggered by a decline. They act to contain the magnitude of a decline, not to prevent one.

NOTES

1. *Economic Report of the President,* January 1976 (Washington, D.C., 1976), pp. 196, 202 (referred to below as "1976 Economic Report").
2. *Historical Statistics of the United States, Colonial Times to 1957* (Washington, D.C.: U.S. Department of Commerce, Bureau of the Census, 1960), p. 9. This volume presents the statistics, where available, for the nineteenth century.
3. Ibid., p. 139.
4. *Economic Report of the President,* February 1975 (Washington, D.C., 1975), p. 250 (referred to below as "1975 Economic Report").
5. "Historical Statistics . . .," op. cit., p. 409.
6. "1975 Economic Report," op. cit., p. 288.
7. U.S. Department of Labor, Bureau of Labor Statistics, *Employment and Unemployment in 1974,* Special Labor Force Report 178 (Washington, D.C., 1975), p. A-32.
8. Ibid., p. 12.
9. Energy prices usually have been lower in the United States than in other industrial countries.
10. It has been noted that "Electricity is not a primary source of energy, but rather the most highly refined form of energy. The energy content of coal, oil, gas, falling water, or uranium can be transformed to electricity, and the history of energy consumption over the past century shows a steady growth in the proportion of these primary energy sources that have been so transformed prior to final use by consumers." John C. Fisher, *Energy Crises in Perspective* (New York: John Wiley, 1974), p. 77.
11. "1975 Economic Report," op. cit., p. 81 and "1976 Economic Report," op. cit., p. 90.
12. The petroleum industry had its start in the United States in 1859. In the first 40 years of the industry's history, we were a substantial net exporter of oil (by 1900 exports were more than one-third of our domestic crude production). Through 1945 we were modest exporters (in that year the figure was 4 percent). Following World War II, the picture changed and there have been large and growing net imports. Consumption rose much more rapidly than output. Sam H. Schurr and Bruce C. Netschert, *Energy in the American Economy, 1850-1975,* Resources for the Future (Baltimore, Maryland: Johns Hopkins Press, 1960), pp. 84-91.

13. "1976 Economic Report," op. cit., p. 7.
14. *Statistical Abstract of the United States, 1975* (Washington, D.C.: U.S. Department of Commerce, Bureau of the Census, 1975), p. 490.
15. See Jules Backman and Ernest Bloch, *Multinational Corporations, Trade, and the Dollar* (New York: New York University Press, 1974).
16. Nicholas K. Bruck and Francis A. Lees, "Foreign Investment, Capital Controls and the Balance of Payments," *The Bulletin*, No. 48-49 (New York: New York University, Graduate School of Business Administration, Institute of Finance, April 1968), pp. 83-85.
17. From 1,323,000 in 1939 to 10,031,000 in 1960 and 11,165,000 in 1972. "Statistical Abstract of the United States, 1975," op. cit., p. 490.
18. Research and development reached a peak at 3.0 percent of GNP in 1965. With declining Federal spending for research and development the ratio declined to 2.2 percent in 1974.
19. Lawrence S. Ritter and William L. Silber, *Money* (New York: Basic Books, 1970), p. 205.
20. Federal Reserve Bank of New York, *Annual Report* (1974), pp. 21-26.
21. See Jules Backman, *Economic Growth, Levels of Living, and the Quality of Life*, an address before the Frank L. Weil Institute for Studies in Religion and the Humanities, Hebrew Union College, Cincinnati, Ohio, February 1, 1976.
22. As the Council of Economic Advisers has pointed out, "Since society places a value both on material goods and on clean air and water, arrangements must be devised that permit the value we place on each to determine our choices." (*Economic Report of the President*, February 1971 (Washington, D.C., 1971), p. 114.
23. *Brown* v, *Board of Education of Topeka et. al.*, 347 US 483 (1954).
24. "Historical Statistics . . .", op. cit., pp. 207, 211, 212 and "Statistical Abstract of the United States, 1975," op. cit., p. 135.
25. Derived from "Historical Statistics . . . ," op. cit., pp. 139, 718-19.
26. "1971 Economic Report," op. cit., p. 116.
27. The improvement of coal-mine safety has involved similar programs. The Federal Coal Mine Health and Safety Act of 1969 contains provisions that "place limits on the amount of coal dust in the atmosphere of underground mines, provide strict safety standards for underground mine equipment, require compensation for miners disabled by pneumoconiosis." *Minerals Yearbook, 1969*, Volumes I-II (Washington, D.C.: U.S. Department of the Interior, Bureau of Mines, 1971), p. 16. The Bureau of Mines was required to make health and safety inspections. The magnitude of investment required as the result of this legislation has been substantial.
28. John E. Cremeans, Frank W. Segel, and Gary L. Rutledge, "Capital

Expenditures by Business For Air, Water, and Solid Waste Pollution Abatement, 1974 and Planned 1975," *Survey of Current Business* (July 1975), pp. 15, 18.

29. John Meyer and Gregory Ingram, "Energy, The Environment and The Economy: Automobiles and Air Quality As A Case Study," in National Bureau of Economic Research, Inc. *54th Annual Report* (New York, 1974), p. 3.

30. Derived from "1975 Economic Report," op. cit., pp. 268-69.

31. Between January 1971 and January 1974 the tax-paid f.o.b. cost of Saudi Arabia oil rose from $1.10 per barrel to $7.11. Ibid., p. 75.

32. President Ford has estimated: "If there is no change in our pricing policy for domestic energy and in our consumption habits, by 1985 one-half of our oil will have to be imported, much of it from unreliable sources." Ibid., p. 5.

33. *Current Population Reports,* Series P-25, 10, No. 541 (U.S. Department of Commerce, Bureau of the Census, February 1975), p. 1.

34. *The New York Times* (July 7, 1975).

35. See Denis F. Johnston, "The United States Economy in 1985: Population and Labor Force Projections," *Monthly Labor Review* (December 1973), pp. 8-17.

36. Herman Kahn and Anthony J. Wiener, *The Year 2000* (New York: The Macmillan Company, 1967), p. 168.

37. "1976 Economic Report," op. cit., p. 195 and "1975 Statistical Abstract," op. cit., p. 6.

38. *Manpower Report of the President* (Washington, D.C., April 1974), p. 31 and "Employment and Unemployment in 1974," op. cit., p. A-6

39. "1975 Statistical Abstract," op. cit., p. 344.

40. In 1974, those 55 and over made up 8 percent of all the unemployed, but 18.8 percent of those unemployed for 27 weeks or more. ("Employment and Unemployment in 1974," op. cit., p. A-14) As the Council of Economic Advisers has indicated: "Older workers are likely to have had much training that was useful to their previous employer but would not necessarily be of value to any other; and because their general training was received at an earlier time their general skills may have become obsolete. Firms are reluctant to invest in an older worker whose remaining work life is shorter and whose retirement with pension is more imminent." ("1975 Economic Report," op. cit., p. 98.)

41. From 1929 to 1965 output per man increased at an annual rate of 2.2 percent in industry and by 1.1 percent in services. Victor Fuchs, *The Service Economy,* National Bureau of Economic Research (New York: Columbia University Press, 1968), p. 51.

42. Robert L. Heilbroner and Lester C. Thurow, *The Economic Problem,*

Fourth Edition (Englewood Cliffs, New Jersey: Prentice-Hall, 1975), p. 309.

43. Donella H. Meadows, Dennis L. Meadows, Jorgen Randers, and William W. Behrens III, *The Limits To Growth* (New York: New American Library, 1972), p. 75.

44. Ibid., p. 29.

45. See the following studies by the New York Stock Exchange: *The Capital Needs and Savings Potential of the U.S. Economy* (New York, September 1974); *The Need For Equity Capital* (New York, February 1975); *Demand and Supply of Equity Capital* (New York, June 1975). See also *The American Economy: Prospects for Growth to 1988* (New York: McGraw Hill Department of Economics, January 1975) and "1976 Economic Report," op. cit., pp. 39-47.

46. Roger M. Blough, *The Washington Embrace of Business* (New York: Columbia University Press, 1975).

47. Because of the slowdown in the rate of increase in the labor force, a U.S. Bureau of Labor Statistics study projected an annual increase of 3.2 percent real GNP from 1980 to 1985. Ronald E. Kutscher, "The United States Economy in 1985, Projections of GNP Income, Output, and Employment," *Monthly Labor Review* (December 1973), pp. 27-42. This projection made no allowance for the energy problem which could mean an even lower growth rate in the future.

TWO

The Growth of the American Economy, 1776-2001

Solomon Fabricant

Professor Emeritus of Economics
New York University

Our glance back and look forward, at the economic growth of the United States, takes place at a time of questioning. As befits an anniversary, we ponder the meaning of our past growth and the purpose of our future growth. In particular, we ask what our two centuries of experience have to teach us about the possibilities ahead; what the value of further economic growth could be, compared with the costs it might entail; and what policies could serve our purpose, whether this purpose is to encourage, or to restrict, or to modify the character of our economic growth.

FURTHER ECONOMIC GROWTH?

To indicate immediately the tenor of my own views on this large subject, let me say what I think about one of the ideas being bruited about. This is the notion that a "slow-growth," or even a "no-growth," economy is desirable, or is in any case inevitable.

With respect to the desirability of growth, I believe it is wrong to aim for slow- or no-growth economy when there remains more than enough pain and hunger to alleviate, and the quality of life for many in this country—and for most of our fellow men abroad—still leaves much to be desired. It is not only economic growth we need, to be sure. The content and the distribution of income can and should be improved. The costs of economic growth can and should be lessened. But stopping growth, or even slowing it down, is hardly the best way to attain these objectives.

I would deny, further, that continued and substantial economic growth in the United States during the years ahead is unlikely. As in the past, we may expect fluctuations in the rate of economic growth. But also, as has been our experience with rare exceptions—and also the experience of other countries—we may expect each wave to advance our economy to a new high level of national output and output per person. No one can say just what the rate of advance will be. We can be reasonably confident, however, that advance there will be, and that it need not and will not be at an insignificant rate.

Despite all the talk about changes in values, the desire for a higher standard of living for themselves and their children continues strongly to motivate men and women everywhere. Despite all the emphasis placed on the pressure of population on scarce resources, the forces that make for higher productivity still operate. I see no end to greater investment in formal and informal education, to the construction of more and better plant and equipment, to the development of new and improved goods and services, to increases in the efficiency with which natural resources are discovered, unearthed and put to use, or to the benefits that greater specialization can bring. To the cultivation of these sources of economic growth, the efforts and enterprise of millions of individuals, acting in their capacities of parents and consumers, workers and businessmen, savers and investors, will continue to be devoted.

To repeat, no one can predict just what rate of growth will result. We can be sure, however, that growth will be greater than otherwise if individuals can plan their futures with the hope and confidence that only sound governmental policies can sustain. These are the policies that enlist and support, not ignore or shunt aside, the forces of private enterprise that have been the mainstay of our economic growth in the past.

I might add that answers to the questions about the economic growth of the United States—whether mine or the answers that others may think more sensible—have significance not only for our own 200 million people but also for the rest of the 4 billion souls that now inhabit the earth. The great mass of our fellow men abroad can look back to far less economic progress that we in this country have enjoyed. Their hopes and fears about what lies ahead are no less poignant than our own. What can be learned from our experience should be useful to them also.

ECONOMIC GROWTH IN 1776

This is not the first time, and we can be sure it will not be the last, when economic growth has been a matter of concern in the United States. The War for Independence was rooted, in good part, in dissatisfaction with the restrictive economic policy of Britain, a policy that boded ill for the future economic growth of the American colonies. Adam Smith, the publication of whose *Wealth of Nations* also came in 1776, pointed to the tensions that were being built up on this side of the Atlantic. No economist can—or should—resist the temptation to quote him:

> While Great Britain encourages in America the manufactures of pig and bar iron, by exempting them from duties to which the like commodities are subject when imported from any other country, she imposes an absolute prohibition upon the erection of steel furnaces and slitmills in any of her American plantations. She will not suffer her colonists to work in those more refined manufactures even for their own consumption; but insists upon their purchasing of her merchants and manufacturers all goods of this kind which they have occasion for. . . . To prohibit a great people, however, from making all that they can of every part of their own produce, or from employing their stock and industry in the way that they judge most advantageous to themselves, is a manifest violation of the most sacred rights of mankind.[1]

These mercantilistic hindrances were not too serious in the earlier colonial years because our economic development was not yet sufficiently advanced to press up against them. Also, little effort was made then to enforce the trade regulations. Smith was clear on this, as on so many other things, for he went on to say:

> Unjust, however as such prohibitions may be, they have not hitherto been very hurtful to the colonies. Land is still so cheap, and consequently, labour so dear among them that they can import from the mother country almost all the more refined or more advanced manufactures cheaper than they could make them for themselves. . . . In a more advanced state they might be really oppressive and insupportable.

Those who revolted were looking to the future. To them the future looked dark indeed when, after the close of the Seven Years (or French and Indian) War with France, Britain began to impose the galling restrictions and taxes which we all learned to recite in grade school: the Proclamation of 1763, which forbade grants and settlements west of the Alleghanies; the Sugar Act of 1764, which restricted the trade of far more than sugar; the Stamp Act of 1765; and so on to the "Intolerable Acts" that followed the tea party of 1774. Given a land with a climate and resources suitable for balanced production—a bold, liberty-loving and enterprising people, made still more independent by the earlier British policy of "salutary neglect"—and a people equipped also with a valuable social, human, and tangible capital brought over from Europe—these basic forces would not be repressed. The American Revolution marked a stage in our economic growth.

Concern over our economic growth continued over the years, of course. I can take the time only to mention the reports by Hamilton, and then by Gallatin (whose "Report on Roads and Canals" has been characterized as "a notable ten-year plan of national action"), the Lewis and Clark expedition, the policies with regard to railroads and later air transport, as well as roads and canals, our remarkable land distribution policy, our public and private support of education, and our continual "quest for useful knowledge." [2]

CURRENT CONCERNS ABOUT THE FUTURE

Recent events have made more acute our perennial concern with our economic growth. One such event is the severe business recession that began in 1973 or 1974, coupled with continued inflation. Fears of a weak or even aborted expansion have been aroused, and there are strong differences of opinion on what to do. Another is worry over the natural resources within and outside the United States brought on by the energy crisis, and marked by indecision over Project Independence and the controversy over petroleum price policy. A third is the intensification of concern over the effects of past and future technological and economic developments on the environment and on the satisfaction derived from work.

The concern reveals itself in diverse ways, ranging from the organic farming fad to the cancer scares; it accounts for the fact that the former National Commission on Productivity is now a National Commission on Productivity and Work Quality. Shifts in values also have been surmised: There is much talk of the decline of the work ethic, and the recent drop in the birth rate has aroused fears—or hopes—of zero population growth. The rise of consumerism embraces many of the concerns I have already mentioned, and others as well. It is not surprising that these various developments, including the appearance on the world scene of successful centrally planned economies or presumably centrally planned and presumably successful economies, have stimulated renewed attention to the idea of national economic planning in the United States. The introduction in the Senate of a bill entitled "The Balanced Growth and Economic Planning Act of 1975," along with the other events already mentioned, reflects the current atmosphere.

THE DIMENSIONS OF PAST GROWTH

The economic growth of the United States can be quickly summarized in a few figures. If we were dealing with a species of animals other than man, we might simply count the number in the population in order to measure its growth. But for the human race we need more. An additional measure of growth (the one I prefer, in fact) is real product or income (the two are essentially the same) per person. And if we put population together with per person product, we have also total national product, or GNP, which is often used as *the* measure of economic growth. Let us look at all three measurements.

Today's population of 215 million is 85 times the population estimated for 1776. Today's real product or income per person is about 18 times the level at about the time of the Revolution.[3] Total product, it follows, multiplied 1500 times over the 200-year period.

Multiples of this magnitude may be difficult to grasp. Let me, therefore, put the advance in per person product, or the key measure of economic growth, in slightly different terms. Over the past 200 years, the volume of goods and services per person in the population doubled every 50 years on the average. Or, comparing one generation with another (assuming the conventional 30 years per generation), the rise between generations averaged about 50 percent. We can begin to understand the generational gap in standards of living that changes of this magnitude tend to create, and the problems the gap may occasionally cause in some families.

VARIABILITY IN THE RATE OF GROWTH

At a time when we have been hearing of the decline in the birth rate, and are all keenly aware of the recession in output from which we are only now emerging, it is useful to recall the variability in the rates of growth in other years. Rather than swamp the text with a lot of numbers, I shall try to extract from the historical record some observations on this variability that can be useful when we try to look ahead.

The outstanding generalization to be drawn from the population statistics is the more or less gradual decline in the rate of increase of population. Population itself never declined, not even from one year to another. However, it grew less rapidly in the twentieth century than it did in the nineteenth, and less rapidly in the nineteenth century than in the eighteenth. The immediate cause of the retardation was a long-term decline in both the birth rate and in the rate of immigration. A long-term decline occurred also in the death rate, but not enough to offset the reduction in birth and immigration rates. In his famous book of 1798 on *The Principle of Population,* T. R. Malthus took the rate of growth of population in the North American colonies as his estimate of uncontrolled population growth. This was a doubling every 25 years. Our present rate of growth—calculated over the past decade or so, in order to average out the recent drop in the birth rate and other year-to-year changes—means a doubling every 70 years.

The retardation in the rate of growth of population was "more or less gradual" because there were many short-term fluctuations. The recent drop in the birth rate may remind some readers of the low birth rates of the 1930s. Many more will remember the baby boom that followed World War II and extended into the early 1960s. Such fluctuations undoubtedly occurred also in earlier decades and for much the same reasons. Wars and changes in business conditions affected marriage and birth rates. Immigrants came in waves, often of extreme amplitude, as economic and political conditions here and abroad changed. And after World War I, when the quota system was introduced, immigration dropped to a trickle, contributing further to the reduction in the rate of population growth. Not to be ignored is the variation in birth rates caused also by the strong random factors that have bedeviled population forecasters. Actual changes in population often have fallen outside the range between the high and low projections made by demographers.

The changes in birth and death rates, and the underlying factors that account for them, have important implications not only for population projections but also for understanding other social and economic phenomena. Obvious examples are the problems of school boards and the increase in the female labor force, not to mention the rise of the feminist movement. Not so well known, though obviously of great significance, is the very large reduction in the probability of children being orphaned while still young, an advance made possible by great strides in dealing with such diseases as pneumonia and tuberculosis.[4]

Retardation in population growth is reflected in the rate of growth of the nation's product, which also grew less and less rapidly over the years. Of course, the growth of national product reflects also the long-term rate of growth of output per person. This, however, has been remarkably stable. There is little or no evidence of a systematic slowdown or a speedup in the rate of growth of output per person where we measure this rate over periods long enough to average out the short- and long-term fluctuations. In any case, a graph of output per capita shows a pronounced upward sweep, as if strong forces were almost incessantly pushing it up. Declines did take place, but only in a fraction of the years, and then they were generally smaller than the increases. As a result, the preponderant experience of our people has been that of increase in family income. It is not surprising that they have come to expect it.

BUSINESS FLUCTUATIONS

As mentioned, the short-term rates of change in output per person and therefore also in total output have not been stable. Their trends were punctuated by fluctuations, and for much the same reasons as the fluctuations in population growth. But the cycles in output and output per person were of much greater amplitude than those found in total population. The range of fluctuation in population growth has been between high and low, but always positive, rates of growth. Not so with output. Even in the postwar period, when business fluctuations were on the whole less violent than in earlier years, and economists had begun to ask whether the business cycle was obsolete (a question since answered by the turn of events) total output almost always fell during a recession. And with population rising even during a recession, output per capita always fell, and by a somewhat larger percentage than did total output.

There are many regular features in the fluctuations in output, as economists have discovered. But there is also a great deal of irregularity, and we should not blink our eyes to this fact of history. The amplitude of some cycles has been small; of others, it has been large. Some cycles have been of long duration, some of short duration. Economists have sought to detect patterns in this variation, for example, to determine whether the more-severe business cycles came at fairly regular intervals, and a large (and largely speculative) literature has developed on the so-called long waves in business activity. The historical record does reveal something like a long wave, extending over 15 or 20 years, that is, a succession of periods of slow and rapid growth. But these waves, like the shorter business cycles, have their irregular as well as their regular features. The record is too scanty to support any simple generalization concerning the long waves. This much, however, can be said with confidence: Periods of slow growth, that is, of relative stagnation, have not become more frequent. The historical record is also consistent with the impression that such periods have not vanished.

ENVIRONMENTAL FACTORS

Because so much emphasis is being put on environmental deterioration these days, it may be asked whether the increases in real income per person cited above are increases merely because we do not make adequate allowance for the seen and unseen costs of environmental deterioration. There is such a bias, I think, but it is less serious than some people suppose. An estimate of growth in real national product in the United States during the period beginning in 1929, corrected for this bias, supports this opinion.[5] It seems people forget that the use of thousands of draft animals in New York City caused pollution before the automobile came on the scene. Cholera flared up in the city on a number of occasions in the nineteenth century. Bituminous coal used to be permitted here. Examples are easy to find.

The sources of pollution are different now, as are the goods and services consumed and the production processes used. And because there is more consumption and production, there may well be more pollution generated, per person and perhaps even per unit of output. But there has always been some concern with this question, and something was always being done about it. There have been improvements as well as worsenings of the environment. The problem arising from the residual effects—the neglected sources of pollution—may be larger now. The concern about it surely is. But it does not follow that the bias in our measures of economic growth makes these measures useless.

OTHER BIASES IN GNP

Another source of upward bias is the exclusion from measured output of "unpaid" household activity. The work done by housewives alone would add many billions if estimated at market prices and included in the measure of national product. Because of the shift of women into the paid labor force and the corresponding shift of household production to the factory and the service establishment, this correction may well have been relatively more important in the early stages of our economic development than in the industrialized and urbanized community of today.

The sharp distinction made in the national accounts between capital gains and current income, and the exclusion of all capital gains—real and nominal—from the measure of national income, also tend to bias upward the rate of growth of national income in the United States. A significant fraction of the income of the early settlers consisted of the increase they expected in the value of their farms as these were developed and as more families settled near them.

However, as in the case of pollution, such corrections as can be made for these biases do not seem to alter seriously the picture of substantial gains by every generation in real product or income per head of the population.

SOURCE OF GAINS IN PER CAPITA OUTPUT

What have been the sources of these increases in per capita output? I have already alluded to the proximate sources of which economists speak. Their rather long list may be compressed into three major groups of factors. One is increase in tangible capital per worker. Another is improvement in the quality of labor. The third is increased in the efficiency with which capital and labor are put to use in production. All have contributed to our economic growth, but in proportions that changed over the years.[6]

INCREASED TANGIBLE CAPITAL PER WORKER

Tools, machines, rolling stock, buildings of all sorts, roads and dams, stocks of materials and other goods, the aggregate of these "reproducible" capital goods, if not also each kind of such goods, has grown more rapidly than the population. This must be so obvious that no time need be taken to muster up the evidence.

It might be said, however, that the supply of land and other natural resources has remained fixed, at least after adjustment for the acquisitions during the first half of the nineteenth century, while population has expanded rapidly. Has not the resulting decline in this "nonreproducible" capital per person counterbalanced the rise in reproducible capital per person? The answer is in the negative. People who ask this question seem to forget that natural resources are natural only in part—hardly more so, in fact, than reproducible capital goods. What we call natural resources are also made by men, working together and using their brains, technology and tools. Natural resources, like reproducible capital goods, can be and have been enlarged.

Consider the farming land in the United State. Trees in the "forest primeval" were girdled to expose some arable land to the sun. Then the trees were felled and the wood removed or burned where it lay. Eventually the farmers would pull out the roots and clear the stones, using both materials to make their fences and walls. Even on the open plains, where there was no tree problem, the prairie had to be broken by a strong team of oxen pulling a special plow.

The same applies, with appropriate differences, to other natural resources. These are the resources the national-wealth statisticians call "subsoil assets." Petroleum? Of course, it has to be there, down in the ground. But it becomes a resource only when it can be reached and extracted. This is made possible by the application of technology and capital. Uranium ore was just rock not so many years ago, but is now counted as a "natural" resource because men have learned how to obtain cheap fuel from it.

The usual measures of land area, then, show a decline in acreage per capita. But when these measures are somehow adjusted to reflect the investment in the land, and thus to take account of improvement in its quality, as has been attempted, these measures do show a rise. There are difficulties in making the estimates; and the difficulties in the measurement of subsoil assets are no lighter, as recent quarrels about petroleum reserves in the United States indicate. However, reproducible tangible capital has grown so rapidly relative to population, that even if nonreproducible capital per person did decline, the sum (or average) of the two would certainly show a rise. For what they are worth, the rough estimates that have been made of real national wealth do indicate a general rise relative to population, and over the period as a whole a rise about as rapid as the rise in output per capita.

HIGHER QUALITY OF LABOR

Improvements in the quality of labor, the second group of growth factors, also represent a form of investment. It is investment not in tangible goods but in human beings, made through education, on-the-job training, and in the provision of better health facilities. This type of investment usually is not recognized as capital formation. Even in the official national accounts, expenditures for these purposes are classified as consumption, although there is some talk of changing this classification. The families and governments that make these expenditures do have other objectives in mind besides that of enlarging the earning capacity of labor. But they have that purpose also, and, whatever the purpose, the expenditures have that effect, on the whole. In that way human capital is built up. The stock of human capital has generally grown more rapidly than population, as literacy and other statistics show. It, too, has been a major source of the rise in real per capita income.

IMPROVED EFFICIENCY

The third group of factors, those that contribute to the general rise that has occurred in the efficiency with which tangible and human capital are used, includes a variety of items. Most prominent, of course, are advances in technology. Another, and separate factor, is the speedier diffusion of advances in technology within and between countries, as transportation, communication, and education improve. Still another is the finer division of labor and greater degree of specialization made possible by the general increase in the size of business establishments, industries, and countries, as well as by improvements in transportation and communication and reductions in tariffs and other obstacles to trade.

A striking example of increase in efficiency and also in degree of specialization is provided by our agriculture. Farm output per unit of total input, the measure of efficiency, is far greater today than it was in earlier years. In addition, the larger part of the equipment, fertilizer, and power input into farm production now originates in mining and manufacturing industries, where it is produced more cheaply than it can be on the farm. As a result, the farming industry that originally accounted for the vast bulk of our employment engages today less than 5 percent of our labor force. Yet it feeds the other 95 percent and provides a substantial part of the world's exports of foodstuffs.

Government economic policy is still another factor. It influences the factors already mentioned, as the reference to tariffs indicates, but there are also direct effects on efficiency. Unfortunately, government policy has often had negative rather than positive effects on economic growth. Protectionist policies, inept tax codes, price regulations, and other interference can severely impede private enterprise. The negative effects of such policies have sometimes offset a good part of the benefits derived from the other sources of economic growth. This is why I stressed earlier the importance of policies to enlist and support the forces of progress, not interfere with them.

INTERNATIONAL FACTORS

The economic growth of our country has been influenced, sometimes greatly influenced, by developments abroad. It is worth dwelling a moment on this fact because it points to factors affecting our economic growth that are largely beyond our control, and in any case difficult to predict.

The diffusion of new scientific ideas and technologies among nations, the international division of labor made possible by foreign trade, the flow of capital and enterprise across national boundaries, the immigration of people who bring with them their "human capital" as well as their other possessions, the attendance of students at foreign universities—all these have contributed in some degree to every country's economic growth. They have certainly done so in the United States. It is true that the formation and accumulation of tangible capital, the enhancement of the quality of labor, and increase in the efficiency of use of labor and capital could and would have gone on even in the absence of these interrelations among national communities. The archaeological remains in the Americas, such as the elaborate irrigation systems of prehistoric Arizona, for example, make this quite clear. But the backwardness of the same Indians in their use of metals and their ignorance of the wheel, before Columbus came, illustrates the disadvantages of their isolation.

What happens abroad can also adversely affect economic growth. The obvious example is provided by war, from which even neutrals usually suffer. There are plenty of other examples, of which a recent and very striking one was provided by the formation of the petroleum cartel and the subsequent increases in petroleum prices. These have and will affect every nation that uses petroleum for transportation, fuel, and fertilizer—which means every nation on earth.

FUNDAMENTAL SOURCES OF GROWTH

In the above discussion I have been dealing with the "proximate" sources of economic growth. They are only proximate because they are rooted in more fundamental sources. These more basic sources are the factors that account for the proximate sources, that is, for the saving and investment that increase tangible capital, the education and training that improve the quality of labor, and the technological and other advances that raise output per unit of labor and capital. The basic sources of economic growth are, in fact, the qualities characteristic of the human race—men's "instincts," to use an old-fashioned term. Men wish to accumulate possessions for themselves and for their children. Men want their children to read and write, even if they are themselves illiterate. Men are "idly curious" and wish to expand knowledge. Men are economical and seek shortcuts and better ways to produce the things they consume. Men are social animals, and they try to build and improve and use their social institutions to serve their public as well as their private interests. These efforts have not always been successful, but on net balance and in the long run, the general result has been forward movement in real income per capita.

ROLE OF GOVERNMENT

The contributions, positive or negative, of government have been classified among the proximate sources of economic growth. But government may and should also be viewed as a basic factor. The role of capital formation, private as well as public, has been influenced in an enormous variety of ways by government, as has also investment in education and health, and the efficiency with which labor and capital is utilized. However classified, the fact that the growth of government activity has been more rapid than that of the private sector must be recognized even in a brief overview of our economic history. In 1900, for example, government employment equalled about 4 percent of the total number of employed workers. It was a little over 12 percent in 1949. And since then the percentage has mounted further and is now close to 20 percent.

To understand this development, it is important to realize, first, that we have a long as well as growing tradition of governmental intervention in this country. Examples were given earlier. To these I add Wesley Mitchell's observation:

> "Rugged individualism" flourished on the frontier. Laws were of slight help to the trapper and the squatter; they wanted little from the government. But the farmers who followed soon began demanding that the government aid them in getting facilities for shipping their produce to market; when these facilities had been provided they demanded that government regulate railroad rates; that government provide "cheap money"; later that government make grants to improve roads, set up land banks, subsidize exports of surplus produce, extend protective duties to agriculture, and so on. When we tell the story of American prosperity we stress the westward expansion as one of the brightest episodes and celebrate the sturdy enterprise of the pioneers that made it possible. But when we study the record in detail, we find the conquerors of the continent full of complaints concerning their economic plight, and insistent with the full force of their rugged personalities that government come to their aid.[7]

Second, public enterprise, as it may be called, is not only a substitute for private enterprise, but also a complement to it. It is idle to dream of an economy operating without a combination of both. "The practical question"—and here I quote Arthur F. Burns—"is not whether the government need play an important part in this nation's economic life, but how that part will be played."[8] Conditions change as an economy develops, however, and the appropriate distribution between the agenda and the nonagenda of government, as Jeremy Bentham put it long ago, changes with it. Much of the vast array of government activities at the Federal, state, and local levels resulted from our economic development and growth. To a degree, also, these governmental activities contributed to our growth, and if not to growth, then hopefully, at least, to the attainment of other national objectives. By the same token, changes in conditions may require the contraction of government activity in some directions. Subsidies, taxes, and regulations that may have made sense years before may now be obsolete and doing more harm than good. This is why President Ford has proposed a thorough review of government regulations.

INTERRELATIONSHIPS AMONG ECONOMIC FACTORS

The enormous changes that have occurred, during the economic development and growth of the United States, in the composition or content of the nation's output, in the distribution of workers and business enterprises among industries and regions, and in working and living conditions have been mentioned only incidentally. The widening role of government is only a major example of these changes. All of them deserve attention in discussions of economic growth, for we can hardly begin to understand the complex interrelations involved in the process of economic growth if we confine our attention solely to the aggregate of national production. Nor can we fully appreciate the problems of adjustment—the costs— that economic growth has imposed and will in the future impose on segments of our people.

An example of the interrelations that exist among the different facets of economic life was revealed by the efforts of economists shortly after World War II to explain how income is divided between consumption and savings. Observing that the percentage of income saved tends to rise as family incomes increase, and that family income had risen generally and substantially over the years, they inferred that savings must have been a steadily rising fraction of national income. They were taken aback when Simon Kuznets' careful sifting of the historical data failed to show such a rise.[9] Offsets to the inferred tendency had to be found, and only then did they begin to take into account the increasing range of commodities and services provided through economic growth and considered necessary for acceptable living standards as incomes rise. This offset was not independent of the general and substantial rise in family incomes, however, in the sense that the latter could have occurred without the former. It is possible to conceive of a rise in output per manhour in the absence of new or improved commodities and services. But the rise in productivity would then lead more to a reduction in work done than to a rise in income per capita. Hours of work have been reduced substantially and vacation time lengthened, it is true. What the supply of new and improved commodities and services helps to explain is the fact that this increase in leisure time absorbed only a modest fraction of the rise in productivity.

PROBLEMS OF ADJUSTMENT TO GROWTH

The urbanization that accompanied industrialization and the commercialization of farming is an example of the problem of adjustment forced upon people, willy-nilly, to the new conditions that result in and result from economic growth. The economic development that increased real income per capita had its aches and pains. It was not a situation in which everybody was made happier, to put it mildly. The very process of economic development posed severe problems of adjustment to new ways of living and working, illustrated by the contrast between city and country. For urban culture is different from rural culture; country mice had to transform themselves into city mice.

Economic development means also a loss of old skills through obsolescence. It was a catastrophe for the skilled hand cigar makers in Manchester, N.H., when they were displaced by cigar-making machines and the semiskilled factory workers who tend the machines. What has happened to the musicians, the share croppers, and the mom-and-pop stores, are variations on the same sad theme.

And there were also the regional shifts. The textile industry moved from one area to another, from North to South in the United States, from the United States to Hong Kong, Formosa, and Korea—and so did the jobs.

For these reasons also, we must recognize that what economic development brings is not all net gain. The gain is "gross," and a deduction has to be made for the adjustment costs as well as for pollution. It is a deduction that would lower the *levels* of real income per capita at *all* stages of development, however. The reduction in the rate of change of income per capita *between* stages must necessarily be less. It can be said, further, that not everyone is pushed out of a job or is forced to move. The younger generation has no skill to lose unless its training is misdirected, and it is eager to learn the new trades and move to the city. However, the training of young people is very often misdirected. The problem of adjustment should not be minimized.

IMPLICATIONS FOR PLANNING

Perhaps even more important than the costs of adjustment implicit in the relative and frequently absolute fall of products and industries, occupations and regions, are their implications for the type of national planning that involves control of production in a detailed way. The origin of new products and processes, the opening of new markets, the innovation of new forms of industrial organization and new ways to finance investment have been very largely, if not entirely, the doing of the private sector. The ideas with which enthusiastic entrepreneurs bubble over can be determined to be good, bad, or indifferent only after risks have been taken and the ideas put to the market test. Satisfying a governmental committee that the risks are worthwhile is bound to be more difficult than enlisting the support of one or another "venture capitalist" hoping to make large profits.

THE POSSIBILITY OF WORLD ECONOMIC GROWTH

Looking now to the future, I expect further economic progress because I expect men and women to remain men and women, and to continue to be motivated by the instincts listed earlier.

But is further progress, as measured by sustained and significant increase in real income per capita, really possible—particularly in the world as a whole—in view of the pressure of population on limited resources? Some would add: Can even the present level of world income per capita be long maintained under these circumstances? Here we are threatened with the Malthusian devil, and here I want to suggest the relevance of what can be learned from the experience of the United States, and the experience of the rest of the Western World, to the problem of the world's economic growth.

THE POPULATION QUESTION

On the question of population, we must understand that what people want are not births. It is children, for the pleasure they give while growing up and the comfort and security they provide when they become adults. When babies survive and live to adulthood, parents will realize, and they did realize in the United States, that it is desirable to reduce the number of births. Children are expensive to "produce" and to rear, even under the old conditions. Under the new conditions of life in urban areas and the higher standards of consumption and education that accompany higher family income, children are even more expensive. And they are less necessary for security in old age than before. The decline in the death rate posed, then, a challenge that was met in the United States and the rest of the industrialized world by a reduction in the birth rate. I suspect it will be met in time also in the less-developed countries. The response may be slow, but it can be helped along and speeded up by education and by the development of cheaper and more effective means of family planning. In this area the aid of the developed countries is playing a significant and growing role.

There is much fear that there is no time, that the solution to the population problem must come now. This fear of overpopulation, or its consequences in terms of hunger and environmental pollution, has been blown up beyond all reason. Even in the United States, there is now an organization called Negative Population Growth, Inc., the initial goal of which is the reduction of the population of the United States to not more than half the 1970 number.

THE QUESTION OF NATURAL RESOURCES

As for resources, here too some lessons of economic history and theory have been forgotten. People complain of an energy shortage, for example. But there is no energy shortage. The price jump engineered by the OPEC cartel does not reflect demand overtaking supply. Petroleum was, and would again be cheap, if it were sold at something approximating its cost. And it will be again, allowing for general inflation, when the price system has completed its job of stimulating supply by producers and dampening demand by consumers, something it has begun to do.

Of course, the price system would do its job more effectively if obstructions to its operation were reduced. The obstructions that result from inept government policies, as in the fixing of natural gas and petroleum prices in the United States, should be revised. Those that result from private efforts to establish, enhance, or protect monopolistic positions, of which examples are reported in almost every daily newspaper, should be fought with stronger and more vigorously applied governmental means. Those that result from the fact that contamination of the environment imposes no penalty on the contaminator require the establishment of an "emissions tax."

THE MALTHUSIAN ERROR

The fundamental error of people who see Doomsday ahead is the one made in 1798 by Malthus. His abstract theory is sound, on its assumptions of little or no change in technology and a fixed amount of land. In such circumstances, the pressure of unregulated population growth is sooner or later bound to reduce the level or real income per capita. Malthus' mistake was in his judgment on technology, a mistake he made, curiously enough, at the very middle of the period in which technology was advancing at so rapid a rate as later to be called the Industrial Revolution.

Since Malthus' time, the mistake of underestimating technological change and the other sources of economic growth has been made frequently. Here, for example, is a statement made in 1945 by two agricultural economists in a discussion of the outlook for world food supplies:

> Food production can be materially expanded on the present crop area by more complete conservation of animal manures, the expansion of commercial fertilizers, the use of more machinery, more efficient livestock, new and improved varieties of crops, control of animal and plant diseases, and more double cropping. Changes, however, will be slow and gradual, with little likelihood that they will contribute much during any one generation. In fact, the expansion will probably be less than the growth of population. This forecast is based on our present knowledge. Of course, farmers or scientists may make revolutionary discoveries. These possibilities, however, have been left to the Jules Vernes.[10]

It will be noticed that every possibility of dealing with the problem of expanding food supply is mentioned by the authors. Yet they simply could not envisage the revolutionary discoveries that were in fact in the making at the time they were writing their book. To them these possibilities were something for Jules Vernes, which, of course, means something hardly likely to happen. But even Vernes might be

surprised to read, as we can read in a recent comment on the food
problem in a publication of the Rockefeller Foundation, that

> There is no technological reason we can't solve it. We've got the
> resources, the land, the water, and the methods at hand to feed
> thirty or forty billion people, let alone four or five. . . . Our
> problems are not technological, they are social and political.[11]

Economic progress in the years ahead, then, is not impossible or
even unlikely, in this country and most countries elsewhere, despite
what the neo-Malthusians may infer from their projections of
population and resources. No doubt the pressure of population is
heavy. The number of "mouths" in the less-developed countries has
recently been increasing geometrically at a rate extraordinary by
historical standards. However, checks to population growth—"moral"
checks—have operated in the past. Knowledge and practice of them
can, and I expect will, spread and operate more effectively in the
future.

As for resources, it is true that Spaceship Earth floats in endless
space, with only a limited count of supplies aboard. But energy is
being continually fed us by our sun, and of more immediate moment
there is man's unique adaptability and inventiveness. What we now
count as resources are but a tiny fraction of the mass of our earth. In
fact, resources, as defined in a valid economic sense, and the economic
yield from resources, have also been increasing, and also at a
geometric, not an arithmetic, rate. And it is a rate that exceeds the
rate of growth of population.

I see no good reason to fear a decline in the foreseeable future in
the rate of growth of resources, and of the income or output they
yield, to a level below or even only down to the rate of population
growth. If sensible policy is followed, if the social and political
problems are solved, the difference between the two rates, which is
the rate of growth of output per person, can be kept high. I do not
mean to belittle the social and political problems that are involved in
choosing and following "sensible policy." The problems are very
difficult. But they are not insoluble. The rate of growth of per capita
output can be maintained even at, or close to, the high rate averaged
during the post-World War II period, a rate that has been as
extraordinary by historical standards as has the post-war rate of the

world's population growth. In a word, looking ahead I believe further progress in raising world income per capita can be made, even with continued population growth. I am optimistic, at least, about the *possibility* of further economic growth.

THE FUTURE GROWTH OF THE UNITED STATES

Now, concentrating on the future of the United States, what may we expect?

We may expect, first, that national product and product per capita will continue to grow. The rates of growth will not be steady; they will vary from one year to another, and sometimes even become negative, for the business cycle has been moderated but not eliminated. The fear of a weak or brief expansion, or looking beyond the present cycle, a decade or so of growth at a pace slower than the long-term average to which we are accustomed is not altogether misplaced. I would not attach a high probability to such an eventuality, but neither would I consider it negligible. It will take some time, for example, before the financial difficulties of the Real Estate Investment Trusts and some local governments, and their repercussions on the rest of the economy, are resolved. We have had such periods in the past. While the stability of the economy has been strengthened, we have not yet learned how to deal with inflation without slowing down growth for a while, or at least, we have not yet come to an agreement on the solution. The possibility of some stagnation during part of the quarter-century ahead should not be dismissed offhand.

We may expect, second, that population also will continue to grow, and at a moderately fluctuating rate. Even if the fertility rate should remain at its present low level, which is insufficient to maintain population, zero population growth would not be reached during the period into which we are looking. In any case, the age structure of the population will change as the echoes of war casualties and baby booms and "depressions" work their way up the population pyramid.

Third, we may expect that the composition of final output will change as new goods and services displace old, as relative prices are

altered, as incomes rise and tastes change, and government regulations affecting the production of individual commodities are imposed
or modified or repealed. I expect, also, that the industrial, occupational, and regional structure of production will be altered in various
ways for reasons already mentioned and other reasons as well.

I could cite here the quantitative projections made by various
official and private organizations.[12] I would not deny value to these
projections. But experience suggests that their value is limited. We
can be sure that technology will advance, but how rapidly and what
the new products or processes or materials will be we can only guess.
We know that tastes will change, but we do not know just how. We
may reasonably expect new discoveries of resources, but where and
when is unknown. And who can predict with any precision the
impact of the outside world on our economic growth?

POLICY FOR GROWTH [13]

Instead of presenting you with an array of projections, therefore, I
prefer to indicate what can and should be done to prepare the
economy for surprises, to strengthen the tendencies favorable to the
attainment of a higher-level standard of living, and to weaken or
offset the factors that tend to interfere with or impose high costs on
production.

Most important, increase in productivity and thereby in family
incomes depends primarily on private investment in training and
education, in plant and equipment, and in the search for means of
raising efficiency. Even in the field of education, where public support
is very large, a major part of the investment is generally made by the
student and his family. This being the case, it is desirable that as far
as possible every piece of legislation and every administrative action,
whatever its primary objectives and whether they be of long- or short-
range character, should encourage, not discourage, consumers and
businessmen to work and to produce, to save and to invest.[14]

Nor should we forget that too little is yet known about the
connection between any given policy and its results. It is therefore
desirable that far more funds than are now available be channeled to

research in the social and administrative sciences and to the improvement of our statistics. Economists of very different political views agree that too little is being spent for these purposes. A recent example is provided by the confusion, for both public and private policy, arising from the very inadequate knowledge concerning changes in inventories. Millions of dollars could be wisely spent to improve this knowledge, for billions of dollars hinge on the decisions based on it.

It follows also that policy should be kept flexible, and new ideas experimental. The possibility of retreat should be kept open. This in turn requires that commitments to keep unsuccessful experiments alive be avoided; and that provision be made for prompt and reliable feedback of information on the costs and benefits of each experimental policy—information to be weighed not by those who may have developed a vested interest in the experiment but by persons who can be objective.

Finally, policy must proceed on a wide front. To try to stimulate economic growth by concentrating attention on just one of the factors or groups of factors that affect production on plant and equipment, or on education, or on research and development, would be wasteful. It would be just as foolish to try to stimulate private efforts to raise productivity and production by using only one of the means available to government tax policy, or financial support, or regulation. No government can afford to neglect any of the sources of economic growth, or to overlook the possibilities of tapping them with any of the means at its command.

NOTES

1. Adam Smith, *An Inquiry Into the Nature and Causes of the Wealth of Nations,* First Edition, 1776, Fifth Edition, 1789, edited by Edwin Cannan (New York: Modern Library, 1937), pp. 548-549.

   (The bibliographical notes are limited to identifying the sources of quotations given or estimates mentioned in the text. I cannot even begin to cite the vast literature on economic growth and development in general, and on the economic growth and development of the United States in particular, to which I am indebted.)

2. The comment on Gallatin's *Report* is Carter Goodrich's; it is quoted in Stuart Bruchey's *The Roots of American Economic Growth, 1607-1861* (New York: Harper & Row, 1968), p. 119. The phrase "quest for useful knowledge" is taken from the title of a paper by Morris Reinhold, "The Quest for Useful Knowledge in 18th Century America," *Proceedings of the American Philosophical Society* (April, 1975).

3. The quality of the estimate of output per capita (or closely related series such as real wages) decreases as we go back in time. For 1800-1830 in particular, the estimate I have used, Paul A. David's, is (as he states) somewhat conjectural. For the period 1776-1800, I have simply assumed a relatively modest rate of increase in output per capita of about 1 percent per annum, on the basis of qualitative information. These bits and pieces of information—travellers' tales, tax, church, plantation and factory records, collections of old tools and instruments, even diaries and Brueghel-type pictures—bear on early, as well as late, conditions regarding the production and consumption of food, clothing, housing, health services, and so on. Care has to be taken, of course, to avoid presuming that restored mansions, such as those in Williamsburg, Virginia, represent the common housing of the eighteenth century.

   If zero change in per capita product were assumed for the period prior to 1800 (an assumption that I believe is inconsistent with the facts as we know them), the multiplication factor cited in the text would be reduced only slightly.

   Paul A. David's estimate of output per capita for 1800-1830, is given in his paper on "U.S. Real Product Growth before 1840: New Evidence, Controlled Conjectures," *Journal of Economic History* (June, 1967). The estimate is spliced to those, for later periods, made by R.E. Gallman and others, and the result presented by Moses Abramovitz and Paul A. David in their "Reinterpreting Economic Growth: Parables and Realities," *American Economic Review* (May 1973).

4. Between 1900-1911 and 1965, the decline in the death rate reduced by almost two-thirds the probability of a husband 25 years old dying before he had reached the age of 45 and his first born child the age of 18. See *Statistical Bulletin* (New York: Metropolitan Life Insurance Company, April 1967).

5. Adjustments of the GNP figures beginning with 1929, to take account of environmental deterioration, unpaid family production, and other omitted items, have been made by William D. Nordhaus and James Tobin, "Is Growth Obsolete?" *Fiftieth Anniversary Colloquiem V* (New York: National Bureau of Economic Growth, 1972).

6. In the discussion of the proximate sources of economic growth I have used estimates prepared by Simon Kuznets, Edward F. Denison, John

W. Kendrick, Laurits R. Christensen, and Dale W. Jorgenson, as well as others. References to some of the major contributions in this literature are given in my article on "Perspective on Productivity Research," *Review of Income and Wealth* (September 1974).

7. Wesley C. Mitchell, "Intelligence and the Guidance of Economic Evolution," in *The Backward Art of Spending Money* (New York: McGraw-Hill, 1937), p. 119.

8. Arthur F. Burns, "Stepping Stones Towards the Future," reprinted in the *Frontiers of Economic Knowledge* (New York: National Bureau of Economic Research, 1954), p. 43.

9. Simon Kuznets' historical study of national product and capital formation in the United States is entitled *National Product Since 1869* (New York: National Bureau of Economic Research, 1946).

10. F.A. Pearson and F.A. Harper, *The World's Hunger* (Ithaca, New York: Cornell University Press, 1945), p. 61.

11. Nicholas Eberstadt in *RF Illustrated* (March 1975), p. 11.

12. If the present age is different from earlier ages, it is not in making projections but rather in making quantitative predictions that unfortunately tend to convey an air of precision. The Bureau of the Census and the Bureau of Labor Statistics, as well as other governmental and also private organizations, have for years now been publishing quantitative projections for the next five or ten or more years on population, real GNP, productivity, and material and capital requirements and supplies, to name only the major items. Economists and statisticians know the qualifications attached to these projections. This is why I emphasize the fact that no one can predict with precision what the rate of economic growth will be during the quarter-century ahead. But few laymen try to understand or even to read the fine print.

13. The discussion of policy for growth is taken from my *Primer on Productivity* (New York: Random House, 1969). For some other sections of the present paper I have drawn on my lecture, on world economic growth, given at Manhattan College in April 1975.

14. Not long ago the President issued an Executive Order requiring every suggestion for new legislation or regulation to include a statement on its probable impact on productivity. How this requirement will work out remains to be seen.

THREE

Government and Business in the United States: A 225 Year Perspective

Carl Kaysen

Director
The Institute for Advanced Study
Princeton, New Jersey

My task, not an easy one, is to give a broad overview of two centuries of the evolution of government and business relations in the United States and, with that as springboard, make a highly speculative leap into the future and forecast how those relations might further develop in the next quarter-century.

In choosing the phrase "government and business," where I might instead have chosen "government and economic life," I mean to indicate a difference in perspective and emphasis, if not in substance. For example, there is no doubt that one of the most important influences of Federal Government activity in the 1830s and 1840s on the economy was the deflationary impact of the sale of public lands. This deflation had a great effect on the business world, but since it was not the purpose of the policy of sale, we think of it as an aspect of government and economic life rather than one of the direct relations between government and business. Similarly, perhaps the most striking feature of government finance in the 1950s and 1960s, when we get far enough away from that period to see it in perspective, will prove to be the enormous growth of government expenditures at both state and Federal levels, on education, especially higher education. These expenditures will have great long-run economic consequences, but again we do not think of them as exemplifying the direct involvement of government in the marketplace and the conduct of business of the kind I wish to focus on.

Now 1776 is, of course, an appropriate starting point for a discussion of this sort for two reasons, one of which you know well. The other of which you may be slightly less mindful is that it was the year of the first publication of Adam Smith's *The Wealth of Nations*. It might be, however, that if I had been free to pick my own time for this lecture, I would have waited 11 years. The anniversary of the adoption of the Constitution, 1987, is the right date for a celebratory review, for the Commerce Clause of the Constitution, in creating, at least in potential, our unified continental market has the best claim to be selected as the single most important act of government policy in American economic history.

THE FRAMEWORK FOR POLICY

To the well-trained neoclassical economist—which I at least once was—the range of issues to be examined is usually formulated in terms of the question: What are the proper spheres of market forces on the one hand and extra-market forces on the other? The framework of philosophical assumptions in which that set of questions is usually addressed is a framework of individualism and, broadly if not precisely, utilitarianism. That framework plus an appropriate set of working hypotheses as to the facts of technology and social organization lead to what is the dominant tradition of economic analysis, namely, that private profit-seeking business operating in the free competitive market provides the most efficient regulative mechanism for economic activity. There is only a very limited number of circumstances that require or justify interventions in the market by nonmarket institutions. Usually these are thought of as interventions by government, and in fact, historically, have been chiefly so, but they are not necessarily so. In another social order or in another political framework, we might be interested in interventions by guild groups of one sort or another. Although there are areas in our society where the activities of such guild groups as the American Medical Association or the American Bar Association have been important, we are primarily speaking of government intervention.

The perspective of the well-trained economist coincides, and not at all accidentally, with the perspective from which this range of problems was perceived in the dominant currents of thought for most of the period under discussion. We might say with only a little exaggeration that the people who made the Revolution and drafted the Constitution did so with the works of John Locke, if not in their hands or pockets, then certainly in their libraries and minds. Locke viewed the main function of government as the protection of property, internally and externally. Adam Smith's list of activities appropriate for government include three: Defense, Justice, and Public Works. Now, Defense and Justice may both be viewed as the protection of property from external and internal threats, respectively, although this is perhaps a narrow view of what is involved in Justice. In discussing Public Works, Smith talked about the need for the government to do those things which were necessary for trade which it would pay no individual trader to do for himself, explicitly mentioning roads and canals. He had an interesting discussion about whether education should be added to this category, and concluded that it should not, as it was better done on a fee for service basis by private entrepreneurs.

Since Adam Smith's day, we have expanded rather substantially the list of categories that justify or demand exceptions to the rule of the market as the major organizing and controlling principle for economic activity, and some part of the following discussion will be occupied with noticing these additions:

(1) education;

(2) the control of monopoly—parenthetically Adam Smith, like most writers of his time, thought of monopoly as something that was produced primarily by government activity and, therefore, the control of monopoly as such meant to him absence of government action rather than its presence—and other expenditures than public works narrowly defined, including research;

(3) in general, the broad class of externalities encompassing economic activities, the costs of which do not fall on those who conduct them, or the benefits of which are not capturable through sale in the market by those who perform them, and theoretically a category that can encompass a very long list of activities, and recently in fact has begun to do so.

There are further distinctions that economists usually make when they discuss extra-market control of economic activities. Typically there are three different aspects of economic activity that might be the objects of intervention and direction by government or other nonmarket forces. First, is the composition of the national output: the list of outputs of concrete goods and services and their prices; the list of inputs and their costs. For quite a long time, economists gave explicit attention chiefly to this aspect of the matter. Second, is the aggregate level of output and its rate of growth. Third, is the distribution of income. These three aspects are intimately interrelated so that change in one always has repercussions on the other two. Nonetheless, enough separation is conceptually possible and practically useful to justify the distinction.

From the point of view of contemporary economic analyses, the second and third items on the list tend to outweigh the first in importance. From the point of view of contemporary business, the opposite tends to be true. Businessmen thinking of the relations of government and business tend more to think in terms of the direct impact of the activities of the government on their own firms and on individual markets and prices. Of course, taxes occupy a particularly salient position in such thoughts. The indirect and diffuse effects of monetary, fiscal, and general tax policies are recognized as great and vital.

It is also useful historically further to distinguish between those kinds of constraints on the private behavior of existing producers represented by price controls, subsidies, special taxes, controls on the use of particular inputs, such as, for example, child labor, and so on, and other controls on business conduct, on the one hand, and the direct provision by government of services, whether for sale as by the postal service or for free distribution, as is elementary education, on the other. Analytically speaking, the distinction between the two may not be important, but historically it has been significant. The change from private to public provision, or, more rarely, vice-versa, has been and continues to be seen as more "fundamental" politically and symbolically than a change in a tax, subsidy or the like.

TWO HUNDRED YEARS

Our threefold classification of aspects of policy, amplified by the division of the first category, can be combined with a division of the 200 years of past history into four periods, to provide a schematic skeleton for our thoughts. The periodization I propose appears to be a "natural" one, although the precise boundaries have no particular virtue. The first period covers the first century, ending roughly about 1880. The second period stretches from the eighties of the last century to the Great Depression; the third period from the Great Depression through the Second World War, that is 1930 through 1945. I shall argue later that we are just now at the end of a fourth period. It is of course customary for a broad historical survey to point to the current moment as the end of a period, and to look forward to an age of transition after which things will be different, usually better; I shall tell you about an age of transition after which things will be different, probably worse.

THE FIRST HUNDRED YEARS: 1776 TO 1880

From the beginning to say 1880, the ideas of Adam Smith and John Locke dominated both thought and practice: the basic notion that government should not prohibit, should not restrain economic activity was very strong. However, this did not include the belief that government should not engage in, subsidize, and promote economic activity.

During the whole of this period, agriculture was the dominant economic activity. Although there was a fairly steady decline over the period in the share of the population engaged in agriculture from over 80 to just over 50 percent, and a similar decline in the share of agriculture in national output, it remained by far the single biggest industry.

The Federal budget during this period was small and it was mostly in balance or surplus. There were some years of deficits, associated mostly with the Civil War. The biggest category of expenditures for most of the period was defense. This may surprise us, but we forget how much the Federal Government spent on dealing with Indians: pushing them West, fighting them, and rounding them up into reservations. That was a fairly continuous activity through most of the nineteenth century, and, of course, we had several wars which also made their contributions. Interest on the Federal debt was second in importance, next to defense. Though it fluctuated widely, it was a relatively big item for much of this period. And finally, especially after the Civil War, pension payments to veterans also was a relatively sizable item. These had the effect, incidentally, of contributing to a redistribution of income from the older East to the newer areas of the Midwest and West; though this was not part of the Congressional intention in providing them.

The major economic activities of the Government were promotional. Up to the Civil War or at least through the 1840s, these activities were state-level activities, especially the building of turnpikes and canals. Relative to the size of the GNP at the time, these were fairly substantial. Indeed, detailed studies of individual states, in particular Massachusetts and Pennsylvania, suggest that in the aggregate sense measured by budgets and the level of activity, "economic interference" by the state was greater in the 1820s, 1830s, and 1840s than it has ever been in peacetime until very recently.

Toward the end of this period, and especially after the Civil War, the promotion and subsidization of transportation shifted from turnpikes and canals to railroads, and from the state governments to the United States Government. There was a mixture of direct cash subsidies and very large land grants; the latter being more important. Those of you who follow the professional esoterica of what economists and economic historians do as scholars will know that there has been an intense controversy, as yet unsettled, as to whether the land grants were necessary in the sense that the railroads would have been built as quickly without them, and even if necessary, whether they were overgenerous, in the sense that the same results could have been achieved at less public cost.

Perhaps three activities of a regulatory or subsidizing kind in this period deserve special notice. The first was the tariff. Starting in the 1820s, when textile manufacturing in Massachusetts particularly and also in other parts of New England grew to sufficient importance, New Englanders shifted from their earlier free-trade views appropriate to a commercial society to the protectionists' views of a manufacturing society; the United States had a tariff on imports of manufactures all through the nineteenth century. In general, its level and scope increased over the whole period, so we had a strong pro-manufacturing protectionist policy. For the largest part of this period, the tariff was the major source of federal revenue.

A second element of Federal policy of a promotional kind of at least equal importance was the sale of public lands. Here again, sophisticated scholars are still arguing the extent to which the policy of selling the Federal lands in the public domain at low fixed prices directly to land speculators and indirectly to western settlers, involved a subsidy and of what magnitude. Their standard of comparison in this discussion is what a profit-maximizing monopolist might have realized on the sale of the same lands.

The other significant piece of regulation was the National Bank Act of 1863. It created a national banking system, but not a central bank. No effort was made in that direction at all during this time. The Act aimed at limiting the extent to which banks regulated only by the states could issue notes, make loans, and accept deposits larger than their reserves could justify. In addition, there was the need for a national currency other than specie. The specific regulatory results, however, and its timing did not answer only to these broad purposes. It was the exigencies of war financing, and specifically the unwillingness of the Congress to let the administration print another issue of greenbacks, that led to the passage of the National Bank Act in 1863.

All in all, looking at our first period, the first century, we can say that some mixture of promotion and public works provided the major theme of economic policy; although the National Bank Act does not fit wholly and neatly under this rubric.

THE NEXT HALF-CENTURY: 1880-1930

The second period—the half-century from 1880 to 1930—shows quite a different distribution of emphasis in public policy. This period falls naturally into three sub-periods: 1880-1916; the First World War, which, from the point of view of our economic involvement and its consequences, reached from 1916 well into 1920; and finally, the twenties.

The first part of the period, from 1880 to 1916, was the most active in terms of changing relations between business and government. First, the underlying economic background changed radically. At the beginning of this period, agriculture still occupied nearly half the labor force and produced more than 20 percent of the national income; at its end urban activities were dominant. In 1880, the urban population was 28 percent of the total; in 1930, 56 percent. In this period we industrialized, and absorbed millions of immigrants in the process, and finally achieved a unified national market. We occupied and closed the frontier, but the ideas of Smith and Locke remained as strong as they had been earlier; there was no serious competitive ideology with wide public support. However, the beginnings of academic dissent from the dominant ideology appeared. Early in the period, the American Economic Association was created as the expression of an outlook essentially counter to the dominant belief in the primacy of the market. The Association was the creation of those academics who had come to hold primarily an institutional and historical view of the economy as a result of their studies in Germany, rather than the dominant market-oriented viewpoint which came originally from England and still ruled there.

During this period, size of government economic activity, though growing, remained small, both absolutely and as a share of GNP. The major items of expenditure, aside from the wartime peak in defense and related activities, were for education and highways, activities which again can be classified from an economic point of view as primarily promotional.

This period, especially its first two subperiods, saw an outburst of growth in Federal regulation of markets. The basis of the regulatory framework under which we currently operate was created at this time. The first short burst of growth was followed by an even more rapid one during the Great Depression; together they saw the creation of almost all of our present regulatory mechanisms for particular markets. No public policy aimed directly at controlling either the aggregate level of output or its rate of growth or at affecting the distribution of income was part of the first efflorescence of regulation. To be sure, the period saw the first progressive income tax, and the Constitutional amendment that provided its legal basis; but income redistribution as such was not its object.

In 1913, the Federal Reserve System was created. Originally it was not thought to be a central bank, and indeed, it was designed *not* to be one. The whole theme of its creation was decentralization rather than centralization. In the twenties, the System began to some degree to act like a central bank because of Governor Strong at the New York Reserve Bank rather than by legislative intent or regulatory wish expressed in the Federal Reserve Board in Washington. Not until the Banking Act of 1935 was it explicitly understood that it was the major part of the business of the Federal Reserve System to function as a true central bank, a lender of last resort, with the consequences for its influence on the level of aggregate revenue activity.

It is in this period that we see the first express recognition of a need for government regulation. Need, of course, is a relative matter. But what we can observe is the first strongly expressed and politically effective demand for curbing or directing sellers on particular product markets rather than aiding them or promoting their growth. In the 1880s the first markets in which the demand for regulation appeared were the utilities, including grain elevators, railroads, gas companies, and street railways. The earliest regulation applicable to street railways and gas companies often was regulation by franchise. The service contract which a muncipality made with a street railway or gas company contained provisions limiting prices and defining service obligations. At the same time, the first state public utility commissions were born and they were concerned with grain elevators, railroads, gas companies, and somewhat later, the first electric companies. It was during this period that the Supreme Court invented the concept of substantive due process, which said that state regulation could not properly have the effect of taking private property without compensation. If that proposition had been literally interpreted, it would have meant that regulation could not regulate, since any reduction of prices or profits as a consequence of regulation could be viewed as an uncompensated "taking" of private property. As a result, the law of public utilities became a wonderful semantic exercise in justifying regulation, yet proclaiming the principle that there could be no "taking" of private property. For more than 50 years, the euphonious but contentless phrase "fair return on fair value" was used as a slogan to justify almost everything and almost anything. As a consequence, a comprehensible rationale of public utility regulation was late in developing and the efficiency of regulation correspondingly degraded.

The first explicit Federal regulation came in 1887 with the creation of the Interstate Commerce Commission. This exemplified the kind of political impulse that was typical of much of the history of all regulation of particular markets. The creation of the Interstate Commerce Commission was a political reflection of the economic struggles of the farmers against the railroads. In a period which was generally deflationary and in which farm prices in particular were falling, railroad rates were not. State commissions could not effectively regulate the interstate activity of the railroads. The generally deflationary atmosphere gave the farmers' problems weight and urgency which they otherwise might not have had, and the railroads offered a highly visible focus for the hostile sentiments of hard-pressed Western farmers. At the same time, the widespread recognition of local and regional railroad monopolies and the record of specific abuses in pricing and other practices provided ample justification for stronger regulation.

The second major item of regulatory legislation of the period was the Sherman Anti-Trust Act, passed in 1890. This legislation was in a fundamental sense unique. It has had its imitations in many Western European countries, and indeed even in the treaty of Rome that provided the basis for the Common Market, but these have all been of recent origin. As a comprehensive attempt to legislate competition as the controlling principle of the economy, the Act marked an essential difference in government-business relations in the United States and in the capitalist industrial economies of Western Europe, both in enshrining competition and in the element of adversary relation between government and business implicit in its enforcement procedures.

The Sherman Act was a product of the same political struggle that produced the ICC; between representatives of Western agricultural populism, who were the victims of deflation, and those of the Eastern financial and industrial establishment who were its advocates. The railroads reappeared as villains and were joined by the oil companies, the producers of farm machinery, the "sugar trust," and other large-scale processors of farm products. The specific form of the legislation, with its two brief substantive paragraphs of sweeping prohibitory language, outlawing "every contract, combination . . . or conspiracy in restraint of trade or commerce" and "every . . . monopoliz[ation] or attempt to monopolize or combin[ation] or conspir[acy] . . . to monopolize" were striking in what one judge described as its "broad constitutional reach." Equally striking was the enforcement procedure it provided: The application of the statute was left to the Federal Courts on the initiative of either the Attorney General of the United States or injured private parties as complainants. Here again, result may well have outrun political intention. Both the broad language and the procedure of enforcement through the courts were products of the processes of legislative compromise. The ingredients which entered into the compromise had contained much more specific proposals by proponents for the control of monopolies by fixing prices and regulating profits as well as the creation of a Commission charged with enforcement. The proponents also placed much of the blame for monopoly on high tariffs, not without justice. The Bill was passed and had no effect on tariffs, which remained high for two more generations.

For the first decade after its enactment, the Sherman Act was not vigorously enforced. In the decade and a half that followed there was an outburst of "trust-busting" that was unmatched in intensity until the period just before the outbreak of the Second World War and the decade and a half thereafter.

The Sherman Act was supplemented in 1914 by the Clayton and Federal Trade Commission Acts, passed in somewhat the opposite spirit from the original. They created a regulatory commission, the Federal Trade Commission, and added to the general language of the Sherman Act a list of specific prohibitions and exemptions. It remains a matter of argument whether these statutes and some of their later amendments (such as the Robinson-Patman Act of 1936) added to or subtracted from the force of the Sherman Act.

Some students of this period have taken the view that the ICC, the Sherman Act which followed in 1890, and some of the later enactments, like the Clayton and Federal Trade Commission Acts in 1914, represented a triumph of the forces of conservatism. In this reading of history, the railroads in fact got most of what they wanted; the Sherman Act did little to inhibit the growth of large business. I think this view has at least as much shock value as interpretive accuracy. For example, the railroads from the first asked the ICC for the right to fix pooled rates; it was denied them. To be sure, they achieved it later in the 1920s, but only in a different political atmosphere, and as a consequence both of wartime control and the first recognition that their rapid growth had ended. Somewhat later in this period, we see the first evidences of new modes of regulation that grew important only later. The first Federal Meat Inspection Act was passed in 1906, in response, among other things to the scandals dramatized in Upton Sinclair's novel about the Chicago stockyards entitled *The Jungle.* Analytically speaking, this was the earliest recognition in Federal regulation of the problem of consumer ignorance: How could the competitive market work effectively if buyers could not distinguish fresh from tainted meat? The Federal Radio Commission was created in 1923 to allocate frequencies on the radio spectrum after stations found themselves interfering with each other's broadcasts, a true case of external costs.

The period provides another example of legislation to deal with an externality in the enactment of workmen's compensation laws by the states. This development has the further interest that it was an early if not the first example of a regulatory program initiated by business, and taking the form of an educational campaign. Compensation for industrial accidents was a matter of state not Federal law. Before 1911, it was governed by the common-law doctrine of master and servant. This placed so much emphasis on the co-responsibility of other workers, "fellow-servants," that in the typical case an injured worker could recover no compensation. Some employers recognized the difficulties this created for worker morale and productivity. The result was the formation of the National Civic Federation that carried on an intense lobbying effort resulting in the enactment of model workmen's compensation laws in 40 states between 1911 and 1920.

These provided for a compensation board to assess damages and award compensation for industrial accidents. Thus the costs of industrial accidents were at least to some extent incorporated as a cost of production that the enterprise had to meet and corresponding incentive to reduce them was thus created.

The experience of economic regulation during the First World War was of such short duration and narrow scope that it left little permanent impress on our regulatory history. The railroads were briefly put under the control of a Federal coordinator, the better to organize the large and unusual movements involved in sending troops overseas. There were some episodes of price control. The Federal government for the first time entered into a substantial role as a producer in ship construction. It proved transitory; most of what the Government produced was sold to private operators, and the Government withdrew from the operation. In this respect, World War I was quite unlike World War II.

The brief interlude of the twenties produced little that was new in the relations of government and business. Tariffs continued to climb; promotion of business was emphasized as the dominant theme of policy. This was exemplified in the amendments to the Interstate Commerce Act immediately after the war, and in the diminution of effort in enforcing the antitrust statutes.

The twenties also saw the first attempt at explicit income redistribution through Federal legislation. In the years after World War I, there was a sharp decline in farm income. Wartime expansion of supply met a decrease in demand, especially foreign demand as overseas production recovered and relief demands disappeared. The "farm problem" crystallized a political issue. Congress responded by passing the McNary-Haugen Bill, aimed at raising farmers' incomes through the creation of Government-held crop reserves; it was vetoed by President Coolidge.

Viewing the second period as a whole, we can say that there was a rough balance between two themes: on the one hand, the continuing emphasis on the promotion of business by direct and indirect assistance, especially the tariff; on the other, the institutionalization in legislation of the recognition that laissez faire was not in itself the guarantee of competition in the marketplace. There were markets in which competition was absent or weak and needed to be replaced or supplemented by regulation. As Adam Smith had recognized, there were markets in which competition was not self-sustaining and governmental oversight was required to see that it was maintained rather than suppressed.

THE GREAT DEPRESSION AND SECOND WORLD WAR: 1930-1945

The third period, between the Great Depression and the Second World War, forms the Great Divide in the history of government-business relations in the United States. Between 1929 and 1933, the Gross National Product fell by half in current dollars and by about one-quarter in real terms. Unemployment, which was not then measured with much accuracy, reached a peak somewhere between 20 and 30 percent of the labor force. World trade between the first quarter of 1929 and the first quarter of 1934 declined 70 percent in volume. There was a slow recovery from the depths of 1932-1933, until 1936, followed by another sharp downturn in 1937. The Second World War brought real economic recovery to the United States, measured in terms of employment as well as output. Some of the European economies recovered earlier and more rapidly during the thirties; our own did not.

The depths of the Depression in 1932-1933 provided an experience of the total failure of the market system that was shared by almost every American. I am old enough to retain a vivid memory of the bank failures and bank holiday of 1933, of the sense of a country in which money had, so to speak, simply vanished, even if only for a short period of time. Whatever glosses and explanations reflection and study later provide, I think it is impossible to exaggerate the significance of that experience as an emotional and political fact.

One result was an enormous efflorescence of regulation. From the point of view of contemporary economics, the problem was the control of aggregate output, of the level of aggregate demand. Few people, if anyone, understood that concept at the time. What was done in that direction as a matter of public policy was quantitively little, sporadic, and, above all ill-informed.

There were two major early attempts to influence the level of aggregate output. The first was devaluation, going off gold in 1933, and fixing a new gold price in 1934 when the official price in the United States went from $20.67 an ounce to $35.00 an ounce. The second was the printing of $3 billion of new paper money; this was done as a by-product of the first Agricultural Adjustment Act in 1933. (The Act was later declared unconstitutional by the Supreme Court.) The problem of the day, as it was seen by the policy makers of the first Roosevelt administration, was a congeries of failures or malfunctions of specific markets. The response was an attempt to deal market by market with these failures and malfunctions. New regulatory commissions sprouted, existing ones were given broader powers. The new creations included the Federal Deposit Insurance Corporation (banking), the Securities and Exchange Commission (stock exchanges and new securities), the Federal Communications Commission (radio and telephone), the Federal Power Commission (electric power and gas). The Motor Carrier Commission (MCC) was created to regulate truck transport and added to the ICC. The powers of the Food and Drug Administration were widened in scope; those of the Federal Trade Commission were also increased. This whole regulatory structure is still with us, a legacy of the Great Depression.

Behind the attempt to improve the functioning of specific markets was a set of broader notions about the relation between behavior in particular markets and the general level of prosperity or depression. These notions were never coherently articulated, they contained fundamental inconsistencies and contradictions, and accordingly they could never be consistently carried out. One of the notions held that there was a relation between the alleged inflexibility of monopoly prices in particular markets and the decline in aggregate output. This view was held by a few economists with access to political power in the thirties and later, although it has never commanded widespread acceptance in the profession. However, it was important at the time, and probably was influential in justifying one kind of regulatory effort. The opposite view—that some markets were suffering from too much competition—was also current, and it too influenced policy. The long series of efforts to raise agricultural prices and thereby agricultural incomes which began in the Depression and has only just ended reflected this view. So did the creation of the MCC, to regulate motor freight carriers, and the Connally Act, regulating the interstate transport of so called "hot oil," oil produced in excess of state regulatory quotas. There may be more respectable professional opinion behind the notion that falling prices in particular markets can have a destabilizing effect on aggregate output, but certainly not to an extent that would justify the policies listed.

In addition to the attempts to improve the functioning of particular markets, the great crisis gave rise to a variety of measures that aimed directly at the redistribution of income and economic power. One such group included the direct efforts of the Federal Government to create employment early in the depression: the Civilian Conservation Corps, the National Youth Administration, the Works Progress Administration. These combined two elements that continue to have persistent force in our economic life. The first sees a role for the Federal Government as an employer of last resort, when the demand for labor by private employers fails to provide jobs for great numbers of those seeking work. The second, analytically different, but practically intertwined, is the role of the Federal Government in providing labor force training, and so making much more readily employable those who by reason of lack of experience, unfavorable geographical location, or other handicaps were previously unable to compete in the private labor market.

The second and most persistent set of attempts to redistribute income centered on agricultural policy. As noted above, the original Agricultural Adjustment Act of 1933 initiated a long series of attempts to raise farm incomes by raising farm prices. A whole variety of devices, deployed in successive legislative enactments over more than 30 years sought to change the terms of trade between the agricultural and industrial sectors in the economy in favor of agriculture. They included Government-held stockpiles in various forms, acreage controls, output controls, marketing controls, and payments for nonproduction. Policy makers and their political supporters rationalized these programs in terms of "excess competition." More sophisticated arguments were possible, and available, but probably were of less political importance in influencing what was actually legislated.

The social security program, another permanent legacy of the Great Depression, may also have been intended as an income redistribution program. It certainly had that effect, especially in terms of the early timing of payments in relation to the timing of contributions. However, at a deeper level it was another recognition of the limitations of individualism and the need for a collective response to a social problem.

The final element of economic policy in the 1930s, that aimed at the redistribution of power and income, had to do with the legal status of labor unions and collective bargaining. The Clayton Act (1914) had earlier specifically exempted unions from the reach of the antitrust laws as "conspiracies in restraint of trade," but the positive significance of the exemption was small or zero. First, somewhat tentatively in the Norris-La Guardia Act of 1932, then briefly and abortively in Section 7a of the short-lived National Recovery Act of 1933, and finally and more permanently in the Wagner Act of 1935, the first National Labor Relations Act, a new philosophy of labor-management relations was given legislative expression. Not only was the right of labor to organize in unions, engage in collective bargaining about wages and conditions of work, strike and picket peacefully, given the sanction of Federal law, but a positive duty was imposed on employers to bargain, and a set of unfair labor practices by which employers had in the past sought to inhibit the growth of unions was defined and prohibited. The National Labor Relations Board was created to supervise the process of collective bargaining and to enforce the legal sanctions that limited employers responses thereto.

The rationale of this policy was in part to give labor more power in resisting wage cuts as a measure of raising consumer income and thus contributing to recovery and in part, a more purely political redistribution of power within the enterprise between labor and management. How much the first aim was realized and to what effect is hard to say. The second one certainly was and has made a permanent change in the American economic scene.

The last item in this recital of the responses of the Federal Government to the crisis of the thirties, was the creation of the National Recovery Administration (NRA), under the National Industrial Recovery Act, chronologically one of the earliest actions taken by the new Roosevelt administration. It was their first full-scale response to the crisis. The life of the NRA was short; the Supreme Court pronounced it unconstitutional on grounds of an excessive delegation to it by the Congress of what the Court viewed as essentially undelegable legislative power. The NRA was a complete and explicit abandonment of the concept of the market as the prime regulator of economic activity. Instead, it created a producers' cartel, or in some cases a producer-labor cartel, for each industry, called a code authority, to which was given the power to regulate output and fix prices and wages. Indeed Section 7a of the NIRA, the first version of what later became the National Labor Relations Act, was the price the administration paid to the trade unions for their acceptance of this scheme. The results, expressed as a "code of fair competition" were nominally subject to the oversight and approval of the NRA; in practice the delegation of codemaking power to industry representatives was almost complete. The NIRA expressed the philosophy that the root cause of the Depression was excessive unregulated competition in individual markets and that consequently, the way to cure it was to regulate this competition through the codes for each industry. In sum, it was an attempt to substitute a species of planning for competition as the basic regulative force in the economy.

After the NIRA was declared unconstitutional, the administration made no attempt to seek a legally acceptable way to maintain the program as a whole. Elements of the NIRA concept entered into the regulation of specific markets discussed above and especially into agricultural policy, but whatever impulse had led the President and his advisers to attempt a wide-scale substitution of "planning" for "unregulated competition" as the central element of policy had evaporated by the end of 1934. Nonetheless, the appeal to "planning" as a response to crisis, seems to me to contain an ideological element of enduring significance, despite the transience of this first embodiment of it.

In sum, during the Great Depression, the first part of our third period, two things were revealed in the realm of government-business relations. First, it demonstrated that the market system could not be relied on with any confidence, and in crisis, it was seen as having simply failed. Second, it showed that a great and indeed bewildering variety of responses by the Federal Government to supplant and supplement the market produced no clear result. One thing which many of these responses shared, especially those directed toward agriculture and the social security system, was to give a significant impulse to the growth of government spending.

The Second World War immediately followed and finally ended the Great Depression. The war brought full, and indeed over-full, employment. It also brought a large measure of Government planning of outputs, allocation of manpower, and control of prices as well as direct Government participation in a variety of productive and research activities on an unprecedented scale. That experience taught or even over-taught lessons almost the opposite of those people thought they had learned from the Great Depression. First, they learned that government action through the instrumentalities of planning and control can accomplish whatever society wishes to be accomplished. Second, there are no economic constraints.

When I say these lessons were over-learned I mean to say that they can hardly be taken as correct as stated. It is certainly not the case that there are no economic constraints. What is the case, of course, is that a large and essentially productive economy like ours which moves from a very low degree of resource utilization to a very high degree—including unusually long hours of work and an unusually high degree of mobilization of the labor force of young people, women, and old people, and other similar forced-draft measures—can in the short run produce what appears to be a boundless increase in output. Whether the first lesson was over-learned is a more complex question, the answer to which cannot be handily summarized in a few sentences. Nonetheless, I believe it a politically valid interpretation of the experience of the relations of government to business in the Second World War which was in many ways as dramatic as the experience of the Great Depression, and one that has continuing force. Finally, the Second World War led to a large and so far permanent growth in the level of Federal taxes and expenditures, which in the long view may be one of its more important economic effects.

THE LAST THIRTY YEARS: 1945-1975

The period we are now in is just coming to an end tomorrow, or perhaps came to an end yesterday—the 30 years from 1945 to 1975. Here again, we have a period of sustained economic growth, perhaps at a rate even higher than that of the last such period from 1880 to 1929. Not only has the growth of the United States been high, it has been fairly steady, and fluctuations in output have been much less extreme than those of the earlier period. The United States became more integrated into the world economy; it trades more and invests more in foreign countries than it has, with a great decline in protectionism. The World War II legacy of a large permanent increase in the size of the Federal budget, as complemented by a large increase in state budgets, Government provision for education, welfare, health, and highways altogether was at a much higher level in relative terms than before. World War II and the period of growth thereafter have also led to a much greater economic equalization of regions and of ethnic groups—except for the large black and Spanish speaking minorities. Our society and our culture, again with these large and important exceptions, grew more homogenized, both economically and politically.

This same period showed a major shift in the focus of business-government relations from concern with individual markets to concern with aggregate output and employment and income re-distribution. Indeed for most of this period, the kind of business-government policy that occupied attention moved from the center to one side of the stage. The centerpiece of economic policy was the Employment Act of 1946, partly the intellectual heritage of Keynes, partly the experiential heritage of World War II. The proposition that economic stability was both desirable and achievable and that governmental action was central for its achievement became politi-cally as well as intellectually respectable. As President Nixon said not long ago, we have all become Keynesians. To be sure, there were some academic dissenters, and there were significant differences in emphasis in the execution of policy at different times and by governments of different political color. Nonetheless, the fundamen-tal proposition that we can and should do something to control the level of aggregate demand commanded agreement over most of the political spectrum.

Further, in the later part of the period, partly under the stimulus of cold-war competition with the Soviet Union and partly through comparison of our own experience with that of Japan and Western Europe, we became concerned with the rate of growth of aggregate output as an object of policy as well as with its level. Intellectually, this reflected the shift from belief in an inherent tendency toward secular stagnation that was strong if not dominant in the 1930s, to interest in the theory of long-run steady growth, which became more and more widespread in the 1950s and 1960s.

Income distribution also became an important object of public policy during this period. At first, full employment and steady growth were seen as the solvents of poverty. All that had to be done to deal with income distribution was to maintain full employment and achieve a high rate of growth. But later in the period, by the mid-1960s, this faith waned, and a great many programs specifically aimed at improving the lot of those at the bottom of the income distribution were tried or proposed. Their novelty lay in the fact that they used or proposed methods other than taxation and the provision of social welfare in the usual way as policy instruments. Particular emphasis was given to job training, including training provided by private employers with Federal payments to meet their costs, and special educational programs for the disadvantaged, ranging from nursery school to college. Another novel and highly contentious element in these programs was what was termed "community action." In essence, it provided training and leadership for those on the margins of society in using the political mechanism to increase what they could get from government at all levels, whether jobs, direct payments, or access to already existing subsidy programs such as occupancy of public housing and the like.

In the more familiar microeconomic area, public policy showed two tendencies. In the early part of the period, there was an increased emphasis on competition, showing itself in a vigorous program of enforcement of the antitrust laws. More cases were brought by the Government between 1945 and 1960 than in the whole previous history of the Sherman, Clayton, and FTC Acts. The Celler-Kefauver amendment to the Clayton Act, passed in 1950, greatly limited the possibilities of mergers among large firms operating in the same or closely related markets. It strengthened the effect of Section 2 of the Sherman Act in limiting the growth of concentration in particular markets.

As another element of the renewed emphasis on competition in this period, the United States became the leading crusader for freer competion in international trade and fewer restrictions on international investment. This posture may have owed as much or more to our desire to see other nations reduce their barriers to our exports and investments as to our ideological commitment to competition. Nonetheless, the several long series of negotiated reductions of tariffs, and, to a lesser extent, other barriers involved further opening of American as well as foreign markets to international competition.

The second tendency, probably stronger among professional economists than in the political world, was to view regulation of particular
markets with disfavor and to talk about reducing rather than
extending its scope. Both the ICC and CAB were widely seen as
inhibiting efficiency, and suppressing possibly effective competition.
The procedural barriers to effective regulation in terms both of time
and knowledge were also given renewed attention.

These discussions ran into the politically awkward fact that the
regulated did not always wish to be freed of their chains. It was
recently proposed that the CAB stop controlling entry and route
structure in the domestic airline industry, and allow these matters to
be determined by competition among the airlines. Economists were
interested and responded with enthusiasm; airlines did not. When the
SEC proposed in 1975 that rules governing competition in the sale of
securities be changed to provide for more access by nonmembers of
the New York Stock Exchange, most members showed less than total
enthusiasm for the prospect. Some welcomed it, most did not.
Nonetheless, the period did show a diminishing belief in regulation as
an effective substitute for or supplement to competition in the
traditional areas of regulation which had developed so strongly in the
1930s.

Toward the end of the period, new needs for regulation were
recognized; especially in the areas of environmental and consumer
protection. They raised novel and perplexing questions of both
externality and knowledge.

In the environmental areas, the basic difficulty lay in the failure of
the price mechanism to reflect the costs of degrading the resources of
air, water, virgin nature, or historic cityscape that until yesterday
appeared to be infinite, unthought of, or unthreatened. Yet, efforts to
incorporate these effects, either by taxes (more favored by economists)
or prohibitions (more favored by politicians and bureaucrats), ran
into equally difficult problems of knowledge. What value should be
placed on pure air, wild rivers, first-growth forests, seventeenth-
century buildings? How threatening was the release of oxides of
nitrogen into the upper atmosphere, or crude oil into the sea?

In the consumer area, similar questions arose. How can we tell
when the medical benefits of a new drug for some, outweigh its
dangers, perhaps, for others. Who should decide, since the consumers,
in one definition, that is, the patients, do not make the choice, and
the consumers, in another and equally or more appropriate defini-

tion, that is, the prescribing physicians, do not take the risks, and perhaps neither has the relevant information.

Despite those novel elements, response to the new demands has largely been by recourse to old and well-born formulae. The Environmental Protection Agency was organized to deal with the new questions in the old regulatory model. The responsibilities, if not the capacities, of the Food and Drug Administration were broadened. A new Consumer Protection Agency is under discussion, to provide information and protection for the consumer of a wide range of products not now covered by law.

Sometime in this fourth period, a new synthesis of government-business relations emerged, and for a time commanded wide agreement in both the political and academic worlds. Its elements were: (1) macro-economic policy for stability and growth as the most important area of government policy; (2) full employment and rapid growth as the major solvent of problems of poverty and income distribution combined, perhaps, with some tax reform; (3) reliance on competition as the main regulator of prices and outputs in particular markets, with vigorous antitrust enforcement, increased worldwide competition through the lowering of barriers to foreign trade and foreign investments as the guarantors of its efficacy; and (4) a diminishing role for regulation in both old and new fields, replacing it wherever possible by increased reliance on competition and the internalization of externalities through taxes, "effluent charges," and the like.

This synthesis was never expressed at any single moment. No single document crystallized it or summarized it; no John Maynard Smith or Adam Keynes wrote its bible. Rather, it was expressed in what another ex-neoclassical economist called the conventional wisdom of "centrist" academic economists, "progressive" businessmen, liberal Republicans, and moderate Democrats over a period of perhaps a dozen years, from the middle of the fifties to nearly the end of the 1960s.

This Smith-Keynes synthesis was far from laissez-faire, in emphasizing not only the need for the management of aggregate demand but also the character of competition, which was not self-maintaining. Yet it maintained a clear separation of macro- from micro-economic policy and thus a correspondingly clear delineation of government and business roles and responsibilities. In particular, it remained consistent with the essentially adversary stance of government to business and vice-versa that had been central to the ideologies of both businessman and populist politicians for a century.

THE NEXT TWENTY-FIVE YEARS

I believe that this brief period has ended and the synthesis failed. We can best look ahead to the next 25 years by considering the reasons for the failure of the new synthesis. First, economists are no longer confident either as analysts or as advocates that they know how to achieve macroeconomic stability, and both the public and politicians recognize and share their uncertainties. Confronting the problem of inflation, rather than that of deficient aggregate demand, the familiar tools are no longer adequate. When both problems appear simultaneously, as they have in the last year or so, the difficulties are compounded. A high level of output may be an unstable level of output. Microeconomic shocks in particular markets, whether the wheat market or the oil market have macroeconomic consequences for the general price level which we find hard to counter on a macroeconomic level. The impulse to respond by manipulation of particular markets is strong. Some businessmen and bureaucrats call for wage and price controls and most economists oppose them. Yet it is a brave economist who is ready to assert that enough competition is achievable in the present institutional framework to place confident reliance on market forces to counter inflation. Only a minority of economists are that brave.

Similarly, the problems of poverty now appear more stubbornly resistant than they did a decade ago. A high and stable rate of economic growth—even if it can be achieved—no longer can be counted on to dissolve the problems. More and more, we recognize the existence of a fairly substantial group in our society that lies outside the market economy, at least as far as income goes. We must ask outselves either how we can bring them within its reach, or whether and how we can extend the nonmarket economy sufficiently to deal with them in a socially and politically satisfactory way.

Neither branch of the question can be given an affirmative answer that commands wide agreement, intellectually or politically.

Finally, at the microeconomic level, there are increasing contradictions between the growing recognition of large new areas of market failure and a correspondingly increased demand for regulation on the one hand, and a growing disenchantment with the efficacy, flexibility and subtlety of the instruments of regulation currently available on the other. These difficulties are especially striking in situations involving new technologies in which future benefits and costs may both be difficult to assess, yet the costs of leaving the assessment to the choices of the marketplace may be high. Consider the decision to introduce a new prescription drug, for example. There has been sufficient experience to justify skepticism about relying simply on producers to strike the balance between the prospects of profit, the efficacy of the drug, and the risks involved in its use. The rate at which new prescription drugs have appeared on the market in the last several decades has been such as to make it almost impossible for the representative physician to devote the time necessary to judge the benefits and dangers of each one, assuming he was competent to do so. Yet, the record of the Food and Drug Administration has not been one to inspire great confidence in its choices.

The difficulty of the problem is further compounded when benefits may show themselves more or less immediately and costs and risks only after a long interval. How can we judge, for example, the wide and effective use beginning 20 years ago of stilbestrol as an anti-abortifacient that permitted miscarriage-prone mothers to carry to term, when the female children so brought into the world now appear to run risks of certain cancers of an order of magnitude larger than those of women in general?

Choices involving environmental risks produce the same kinds of puzzles, the more so that some of them must be made on a much larger all-or-nothing scale. Is it wise to allow the reprocessing of the uranium fuel of fission reactors, before the problems of safety and security involved can be resolved? Can we learn to resolve them in advance of the decision? Is the risk that use of the convenient aerosol spray can will result in the destruction of a significant fraction of the ozone shield well-enough understood and large enough to justify a prohibition of their further manufacture?

We may ask the more general question as to whether the difficulties exemplified simply can be resolved by raising the level of competence of the agencies now responsible for them, or whether they reflect deeper problems of the limitations of the adversary mode that presently relates the business firm proposing to introduce a new product or process and the government agency regulating or licensing it as a framework for reaching decisions of this sort.

Further, many of our new technologies require decisions of the kind that current mechanisms seem incapable of making. This is particularly true for the class of decision involving the location of large-scale mining or manufacturing facilities, which are on the one hand essential, and on the other seriously damaging to the environment. We have long since rejected the notion of an unregulated market in land as the only mode of making such locational decisions, constraining the market by various land-planning and zoning instrumentalities, usually at the local level of government.

The question of how much more of our finite shoreline should be given over to refinery sites, for example, cannot be settled efficiently at the local level of decision, or even at the state level which is as broad a scope for such decisions as our present legal institutions provide. We have no national mechanism that can decide how much more the citizens of New Jersey should be required to give up in the way of local amenities in behalf of the citizens of the Northeast in general, or of the nation as a whole. Similar problems arise in connection with the siting of large power stations, nuclear or conventional, the exploitation of coal reserves by strip-mining, the extraction of oil from oil shale, or the processing of other very large bodies of low-grade minerals.

Choices of this sort can be made rationally only on a national level, or at least within some framework that permits them to be seen in a national perspective. Today, there is no body short of the Congress that possesses the scope of authority to make them, and the Congress seems an especially poor instrument for making them rationally, or even at all. The same can be said for decisions concerning the acceptance or rejection of new technologies, with potentially large benefits and risks, both highly uncertain.

All in all, the familiar boundaries that separate what business and the market can and should do, and what government must do seem to be dissolving. One set of responses to this changing situation is to deny it; that remains the majority, although not the unanimous, response of my profession. Those in the economic profession who see the new synthesis as still valid far outnumber the critics and skeptics. Among the minority of dissenters there is a smaller but growing minority calling for some form of national planning; they probably find wider sympathy amongst the politically active population outside the profession than within it.

A second response, which has been characteristic of the liberal elements in the business community and is exemplified by the Committee for Economic Development, is to call for the assumption by business and trade unions of responsibility for the broad social consequences of their actions. Many critics of this view have rejected the possibility of business effectively assuming these social responsibilities on a voluntary basis. A few in consequence have asked for greater public participation in the processes of corporate decision-making on issues of the kind here discussed. Christopher D. Stone's *Where the Law Ends* gives a forceful presentation of this view.

We can begin our speculation as to which of these tendencies will prevail in the next chapter of our story of government-business relations by remarking on the continuing changes in the context within which our own economy and polity function. As compared with its position in the world of half a century ago, the United States stands near the extreme of "freedom" among market economies. Only a few of the small, internationally open trading economies, such as Hong Kong or Singapore, are freer from control and regulation. On the whole, the economies of the larger societies organized on market principles show a much greater level of government controls of more far-reaching scope than our own. Further, societies organized substantially on market principles constitute a smaller part of the total world economy, and certainly contain a smaller fraction of the world's population than they earlier did. And, among these, those living under a well-established rule of law with respect to both personal liberties and property rights constitute a fraction of the total.

In our own society, composition of output has been moving in favor of products and services not traditionally organized in enterprise and market terms, such as education, health, care, and public amenity, and this is true of industrial economies in general. Not all of these are necessarily provided by the State, but they all do increase the scope of nonmarket principles as organizers of social activity, and thus disseminate the lesson that things can be done that way.

Further, the mechanisms of democratic politics increasingly generate pressures for sharing the costs of economic change in a "fair" way, rather than accepting their initial unequal incidence as determined through the market as inevitable. Unforeseen shifts in demand or relative prices, interruptions of supply, or technological failure, the initial effects of which appear in industrially or geographically concentrated unemployment, give rise to strong demands for government intervention to distribute the burdens of adjustment more fairly, which concretely usually means more widely. Governmental attention to control or restraint of inflation raise particularly acute issues of equity; the costs of macroeconomic restraint vary widely in their microeconomic incidence. Yet social groups particularly affected grow less willing to accept their extra burdens and have access to increasingly effective means of giving their resistance politically significant expression.

CONCLUSION

In my judgement, these forces will make our fifth epoch of government-business relations one in which the sphere of purely private market-oriented business decision will shrink further. What will grow correspondingly will not be primarily the currently familiar apparatus of formal government regulation expressed in new statutes and new governmental regulatory agencies. Rather it will be some mixture of two elements that are still novel for us, though much more familiar in the capitalist societies of Western Europe. The first will be changes in business structure and governance that will give scope for and weight to representatives of public and labor constituencies to influence the decisions taken within the corporation. The second will be a growth in governmental and quasi-governmental "planning," most likely of an informal or indicative type, rather than under formal legal sanctions. This, in turn, will alter significantly the environment of information and expectation in which corporation decisions are made.

If these changes in fact occur, an inevitable consequence will be the diminution of market competition in the business world, or, at least its transmutation into forms that would now seem unfamiliar and unbusinesslike.

These changes might reach far enough so that an observer in 2025 could say that by the beginning of the twenty-first century, the Organic State had finally replaced the vanishing Umpire State in all the major societies of the world. But again, they may not. Institutions and societies develop not according to their inherent logic, as seen from one or another particular perspective, but in response to the ever shifting array of forces of the moment, which attain clarity and continuity only when viewed ex-post.

FOUR

Economic Life in America
and the Corporate Contribution

Roger M. Blough

Former Chairman
United States Steel Corp.
Partner
White and Case

In appraising the role of corporations in our nation's economic growth let us briefly backtrack 200 years, to 1776.

By present-day standards the 13 colonies, soon to become states, constituted economically a seriously underdeveloped nation. In those days corporate life, to the extent it existed at all in the colonies, might be termed barely embryonic. In the intervening 200 years multiple and massive changes have occurred in our nation, in our way of life, and in our economic environment. Much of that change occurred because of, or concurrent with, the startling rise of corporations of all kinds, sizes, and variable utility.

Whatever our nation's current problems may be, it has without question become the premier industrial nation of the world with, in my view, ample latitude for far-reaching improvements.

While evaluating past contributions is of keen interest, it is the present and the near-term future which holds our attention. Thus, with some necessary disciplines, we will also focus on the political environment to which corporations may look forward, and the effect of that environment on national production or, to put it differently, the effect on our nation's abundance and its competitive strength.

GROUP ACTIVITY AND ECONOMIC GROWTH

Picture the early situation from a production and corporate point of view. In 1776 there were only about 3 million widely scattered people in the 13 colonies. The first census in 1790 estimated about 3.9 million people, with over 3.5 million, or more than 90 percent, living outside of cities and mostly engaged in agricultural pursuits. The larger cities, Boston, New York, and Philadelphia, were in reality small towns.

Commercial activity was largely accomplished by single-owner-ship, single-purpose proprietorships. There were scatterings of small partnerships but stock companies in the colonies were practically nonexistent; the situation was the same abroad although a few trading and shipping companies did exist. In the colonies there were only a few mutual fire insurance companies, one started before the revolution, a second in 1784, and two stock insurance companies two years later. There were also a few turnpike and canal companies together with some toll bridge companies. The Bank of New York, established under the leadership of Alexander Hamilton, gives its birth year as 1784. George Washington, it is said, was involved in the Potomac River Company organized about 1784 to build canals. There were also a few private bankers, including Robert Morris in Philadelphia. And even though Ben Franklin was a very important citizen with substantial interests he did not use corporations in operating his businesses.

The Revolutionary War was a general uprising of freewheeling individualists seeking removal of restraints from the mother country. There were literally no corporate organizations around to be called on in that struggle. With the fetters to England severed and with the organization of the state and Federal peacetime governments, something new was added, inhibitions were removed and a new era in the organization of human effort began.

Projects began to spring up. Many were too large to be handled by single proprietors or even by loosely managed partnerships. Practical circumstances caused the new nation to turn gradually toward forms of corporations which could issue stock. This type of organization had a number of advantages. A farmer with savings to invest could keep on farming while his savings went to work in a stock company. Unlike a partnership, the company did not terminate or require reconstitution on the death of a partner. Stock was transferable. When so provided, stock carried no liability for the losses of the enterprise to the stock's owner other than the value of the stock.

Moreover, the size of the jobs that needed doing began to increase. Larger water companies were organized. In New York City, following a yellow-fever epidemic and a futile attempt to create a municipal water company, the City Council entrusted the task of supplying water to a private corporation. On March 27, 1799 a bill to create the Manhattan Company was presented to the state legislature and passed seven days later. This company had capital of $2 million, a board of 12 directors, and legislative sanction also to become involved in "monied transactions or operations not inconsistent with the Constitution and laws of the United States." This it did. Soon it was in the banking business and a few years later stopped supplying water. Eventually it became a part of Chase Manhattan Bank.

As this example illustrates, larger tasks involved more people and the need to assemble more capital. Shipbuilders found a market offshore for their ships. Larger amounts of temporary financing were needed on the major projects. The stock company lent itself to the efforts of people to organize in sufficient numbers and with sufficient financial strength to go forward with larger projects.

ORGANIZING HUMAN EFFORT

Colonists were not unacquainted with organization or its values. They had simple forms of organized government, including the equivalent of states, towns, and townships. A colonial church was an organization. They understood the natural advantages of various forms of organization which existed among Indian tribes or among wildlife such as geese winging north in formation. They and their ancestors knew animals grazed in herds and hunted in packs to their mutual advantage. Military matters were organized efforts. The Philip of Macedonia phalanx was an historic example. So it came naturally to organize to accomplish the new types of work projects that were constantly needed. Moreover, it seemed advantageous to turn to the limited liability stock company, the most convenient form of mutual cooperation they could then devise.

In fact, rather than ponder the contributions of corporations as such to economic growth in America, it would be perhaps more accurate and understandable to portray economic developments in terms of the effectiveness of organizing human effort. In effect, groups of people became more organized as the nation's tasks grew in number and in size. In a sense, then, men and women with initiative organized themselves into groups which were largely responsible for the nation's economic growth. The corporate form they adopted lent its great workhorse role as a convenient way of accomplishing their respective group tasks.

In any event, business units were born. Small at first, but gradually increasing in size as the tasks to be performed changed in magnitude and complexity.

Organizing group activity was not as easy in the early days as it is today. The state legislatures, when called upon to grant a corporate charter, frequently acted sparingly with respect to the privileges granted to a water company or a banking company or a bridge company. As the legislators became more familiar with the fact that the corporation was the best means to a desired end, the laws were improved and the requirements eased. New York State enacted a law providing for the granting of general charters in 1811 and Massachusetts a law in 1830 granting limited liability.

VENTURE CAPITAL

From the outset a major need to get on with the many projects was to seek funds from investors. Assembling capital was, of necessity, almost a neighbor proposition. There were no capital markets as we know them, although in 1792 a group of merchants and auctioneers began to meet daily to buy and sell securities under a buttonwood tree on Wall Street. Also before too long funds could be borrowed from abroad.

Supplying venture capital was not a new idea. Queen Isabella is said to have sold her jewels to enable Columbus to assemble ships and men and supplies for his projected voyage to the Far East which ended in what was later called America. The India Company and other old world trading companies were also examples of capital aggregation.

One of the early developments in the new nation was the railroad. Steam locomotives and the metal rail made it possible, first in England and then in the United States in the 1820s. The oldest locomotive in the United States was the Stourbridge Lion, now on exhibit in Honesdale, Pennsylvania. It was built in England and began operating here in 1829. With the growth of railroads in the East and Middle West, the transcontinental railroads soon followed, with the first track completed to the West Coast in 1869. The nation assisted the whole development with large Federal land grants.

Unfortunately, aggregating capital caused problems as well as benefits. Scandals in connection with securing capital for building railroads involved misrepresentation, exorbitant commissions, and misuse of funds. These financial activities made a decidedly unfavorable impression on investors and the public. Thus arose the need for investor protection. Yet it must be noted that however the money was raised, the much needed railroad transportation was accomplished with the help of growing numbers of investors.

THE INVENTIONS, THE MEN, AND THE METHODS

In this brief recital it requires a massive exercise of self-restraint to limit to feasible proportions the experiences of what might be called the nation's "middle years" in economic growth. There is so much to explore. Some of the areas of keenest interest to me include the part played by physical inventions. Another area of interest concerns the many industries which grew up in the new nation partially as a result of inventions. For example, the railroads mentioned earlier and the telegraph systems beginning in 1844, and the telephone networks beginning about 1876, and the processes of providing the electric light first in 1879 and electric power for America. Or the massive strides in iron and steel production which started in this country about 1644 on the Saugus River in Massachusetts. And the rise of the great automobile and truck manufacturers.

Mention must be included of the building over those 200 years of strong and highly serviceable banking and finance institutions. Also later came the radio and television industries, the sizeable business machine and data processing industries, and the ever growing service groups. Nor can we fail to mention in this necessarily abbreviated list of industries the many faceted publishing industry with its news-papers, magazines, books, and other forms of printed commu-nications.

Moreover, it would be almost tragic not to spend at least some time considering such gifted individuals as Eli Whitney, credited with inventing the cotton gin, which had such a revolutionary effect on the South and on the use of cotton. Before that, as early as 1798, he was perhaps the originating practitioner of the new technique of the interchangeable part in producing firearms and other manufactured products.

There was also Samuel F. B. Morse, the talented originator of the telegraph system, and Alexander Graham Bell in the telephone field. Thomas Alva Edison, with his whole gamut of phonograph, motion picture camera, and electric light inventions surely must be included in the list of the great inventors.

Then there was Isaac Merrit Singer, and the sewing machine he invented in 1851 utilizing earlier needle and lock stitch inventions of Elias B. Howe. And consider our modern nuclear developments, with such inventive adventures as landing on the Moon. To name one individual or one invention in almost any category is, unpardonably, to do injustice to others.

Still another area is comprised of the group leadership in the industries which evolved. In addition to the individuals named, there was Carnegie, and Schwab, and Gary in steelmaking. There was John D. Rockefeller in the oil industry. And Henry Ford, Alfred Sloan, and Walter Chrysler in the automobile industry. And Firestone and Goodyear in rubber. And Thomas Watson in the business machine area. And Sarnoff in radio and television. And J. P. Morgan, among many others, in banking and finance.

Each built on the achievements of others before him. Yet, in sum, it is a truly amazing aggregation of gifted individuals in the business world who have come and gone over those 200 years, leaving behind an imperishable legacy. Most of them started alone or with relatively small organizations but soon were forced into utilizing larger business units, assembling skilled people who worked with a common purpose and with aggregated capital as one of their tools of production.

Great, therefore, as the inventions were and the leaders of industrial development, translating that leadership and those inventions into the nation's economic growth depended on group activity. Brilliant as the contributions of these uncommon individuals may have been, and important as they were in bringing about organized groups, it was organization that counted most. I count as extraordinary the contribution over the years of the improvements in group activity techniques, or, if you please, in management.

There are so many ways to evaluate contributions of productive groups over the years. How did they become organized? How did they learn to produce to the greater advantage of their counterparts in other groups as well as their own? How did they compete, recognizing, of course, that the competition was imperfectly achieved in many cases?

I realize that simplistically showing how corporations tended to originate is not the equivalent of demonstrating their role in the economic growth of the nation. It is equally true that whatever their role in the past, they may or may not be performing an adequate service today. They must continuously answer the nation's question, "What have you done for me lately?"

Nevertheless, when we evaluate the nation currently, we must concede its monumental economic growth. No one endowed us with automobiles, highways, or airplanes, or electronic systems, or hospitals, or homes. A system of accomplishment must have been present. And that is where the people groups with aggregations of capital come in. Few realize that about 83 percent of nongovernmental activity is done through corporate business units.

FARMING AS AN ILLUSTRATION OF ECONOMIC CHANGE

Illustrating the economic contributions of the nation's multifaceted production systems is not easy. I thought perhaps the complex accomplishments in the farming area would be a comprehensible and instructive yet notable example. In 1776 about 90 people in every 100, more or less, were engaged in farming. In the early days our forebears, working with the tools and knowledge they then had, were in effect feeding themselves but few others. By 1925 about 30 percent of American workers were still in some phase of agriculture. In 1953, one worker in seven was living on a farm and with the equipment and processes then available was able to supply food for 16 persons.

Today only one in 22 persons lives on a farm, and currently each farm worker provides food for about 55 humans. Certainly something new has been added. You may speak of farm machinery or fertilizer. But the best way I know to describe the added ingredient is to call it organized group activity.

Few of us realize that in 1974 the invested capital per farm worker was more than $90,000 compared with about $30,000 on average for his industrial counterpart. Clearly, something has changed in farming in the last 200 years and notably in recent times. That change is still going on.

I suppose farming is one of the most "nongroup"- or small-group-independent forms of earning a livelihood. Yet farming is completely dependent for its excellent record upon the products of many nonagricultural organized groups. Consider for a moment the various forms of equipment used to till, fertilize, and plant the soil and then harvest the resulting food product. Think not only of the groups of employees building the great harvesters now being utilized but also of the many back-up groups mining the ores and coal that move over railroads to steel mills to be made into steel and then moved again to the manufacturer of farm equipment. Consider the sources of fuel for the farm and the transportation needed.

Farmers also have multiple needs for all forms of capital, from mortgages to inventory loans to installment purchases of equipment.

The farmer is as dependent on groups of other workers as they are on him. But with the advantages of group activity, freely doing what each finds to do and improving today on what it did yesterday, we all manage somehow to get on with our work and, with due apologies to our pockets of low incomes, get on with our national abundance.

This is one example of economic growth but there are thousands of other categories of development that would show equally amazing results.

THE SECRET OF ECONOMIC DEVELOPMENT

Was there, you may ask, any one secret during the 200-year economic explosion which gave the United States more or less abundance and something of an edge?

I suppose one may list many things, such as personal freedom, stability of our form of government, our constitution, the multistate commerce clause, the large population growth from internal sources and from an influx of people from abroad, the free access to educational facilities, and the excellent means of communication. There were abundant natural resources although some other nations have relatively as much or more. All have contributed, as well as the work ethic of our many peoples and, not to be neglected, the freedom afforded by the market philosophy of Adam Smith and the limited governmental participation in the marketplace proposed by the philosophy of John Locke.

But I would like to give an emphasized credit for economic results to the freedom of group organization, and the freedom of interplay between the groups, and the freedom of initiative within a group.

GOVERNMENT REGULATION

It was no oversight that I failed to list, among the major contributors to our economic results, our recent governmental massive rule-making and regulatory processes as well as our national planning of one sort or another.

Let us look at that side for a moment.

As the population grew, the working groups we call business units also grew in size and complexity. This growth was fathered by the many new inventions and work processes, many man years devoted to research, and the avid thirst on the part of producing units and the insatiable desire on the part of most people for a safer, more convenient, more satisfying life with at least an element of leisure. The process was fueled by the profits generated.

But as one would expect, with the growth in population, in size of productive units and the complexity of living generally, the numbers of rule makers and the numbers of rules also grew.

In the last 20 years there were at least 104 new laws further regulating business. They ranged from ecological restrictions, such as the Clean Air and Water Acts and the Noise Control Act, to such laws as Economic Stabilization, Occupational Safety and Health Act, to the recent Pension Act, and many others.[1] And the halls of Congress continue to resound to more new legislative proposals and the impetus for more new laws seems almost irresistible.

THE RISE IN RULE MAKING AHEAD

Like it or not, we are destined to see a rise in governmental rule making. And business regulations have strong propensities for fostering more regulations as well as interpretations of regulations. All in all, corporations are witnessing—more accurately, corporations are playing a somewhat tragic role on the receiving end of—an embracing governmental tide of regulations at the national, state, and local level.

Whatever other attributes this regulatory tide may have, when we look at the past 200 years and witness the pulsating economic growth of the country, it will be recognized that growth occurred in the presence of the many favorable conditions indicated, not the least of which was the flexibility of group activity. However, daily that flexibility, that ability to move from origination to operations, becomes more restricted. Yet a vibrant, researching, competing business unit is, among our national assets, one of first importance.

Certainly social ends must be accomplished. But production is also a vital social end. In an expanding economy, employment which accompanies production serves an indispensable social end.

PUBLIC SCRUTINY AND CORPORATE CRITICS

But corporations are not without their critics, and these days we engage, as we should, in pointing out the shortcomings of the independent group method of production, and of the never-enough achievements of the respective groups. We claim a given industry commits unforgivable environment blunders or that this or that group does not try hard enough to employ all the right people on an equal opportunity basis or permits its work environment to become virtually a special Hades. We spend many hours discussing the tax aspects of group activity. "Do they pay enough?" we ask. We get concerned, or overly concerned, with size and something we call corporate power. We regulate this and restrict that.

And not too long ago we heard that production as practiced in this nation is a form of selfish profit seeking with direct detrimental effects on the public at large and, therefore, we were told, "Please take the emphasis off new gadgets, new cars, new foods, new drugs, and more of everything for everybody." Perhaps I listen to the wrong people, but I seem to hear less of this pattern today than, say, five or ten years ago.

Nevertheless, recognizing the rather remarkable role of the various kinds, sizes, and economic contributions of corporations in our nation's growth does not and should not translate into an immunity from constant scrutiny. This public scrutiny or examination of the function and value of corporations and their managements goes on constantly and sometimes intensely, as I think it should. In essence, public scrutiny of business units is the people examining themselves and their performance, since most of them are in or dependent upon business units.

In the Great Depression of the thirties a reexamination of economic health produced such statutes as the National Recovery Act and the Acts administered by the Securities and Exchange Commission. And the theme of exercising direct centralized government controls over major business units recurred but did not then produce a direct legislative result. Another effort in the 1950s also was fruitless.

Recently, a further and multiphased attempt has been initiated by various sources to consolidate in the Federal Government controls of business units, especially large corporations. It has superficially a broad appeal. Proponents of such regulatory causes as consumerism, job safety and health, equal employment opportunity, and the advocates of greater corporate disclosure generally feel a desire to support either Federal incorporation or Federal standards to govern corporate conduct.[2] Having the Federal Government rather than the 50 states do it is at once, they think, an easy way to accomplish their control purposes and at the same time it gives direct access to the mechanics of controls.

FEDERAL STANDARDS FOR CORPORATIONS

Federal standards for corporate conduct or Federal incorporation are usually based on several types of recurring criticisms. One relates to the alleged inability of any state, for example Delaware, to protect stockholders and consumers from a corporate management which operates in many states and, perhaps, internationally, and which is claimed to be insensitive to the public welfare.

Another criticism is based upon broader considerations than stockholder protection. Here again the charges are made against the larger corporations. These, it is said, are centers of too great power with too much impact on production, employment, prices, discrimination, and environment. Lately, moreover, the ethical standards of the conduct of corporate business at home and abroad are being criticized.

To open or close a plant, to offer employment or disengage employees, to raise prices, to advertise products thought by someone to be unwanted or unnecessary may have socially undesirable by-products, it is said.

The further criticism is made that existing legal structures such as antitrust laws or environmental standards are either too laggard in execution or too inadequate. Moreover, standards of personal liability of executives and sanctions generally fail to exert the necessary restraints.

The solution, some critics say, is to require either Federal incorporation or enactment of new Federal standards for corporations. It is recognized that Federal incorporation itself is a form of setting Federal standards and a ready method of applying Federal sanctions through the ability to withhold or withdraw approvals of corporate existence.

The details of the various proposals, some of which are yet to come, range widely. For example, disclosure of sales and profits by product line is put forward as a requirement that encourages competition. The environmental standards will take on much broader and more detailed dimensions, permitting promulgation of detailed controls required less by statute than by edicts of commissions. Vigilant citizens groups would have the right to peer over the shoulder of enforcement agencies, supplementing such enforcement with legal actions of their own. Corporate management would be under the direction of boards composed of so-called consumer and public representatives as well as directors representing the stockholders. The number of directorships held by a single individual would be restricted.

Along with more stringent standards for a director's conduct would come nonmonetary penalties for conduct determined to be improper. One discussed is disbarment as a director. Current indemnification against liability of directors would be narrowed.

Various new requirements for stockholder approvals would be generated. The size of corporations would be preordained. In a word, although clothed in innocuous garments, the Federal standards—Federal incorporation movement can represent virtually a fundamental reordering of the nation's economic system.

How would this differ from what we have? The answer is in the massiveness of the regulatory process and in the increased centrally directed decision making. Under current corporate practice, whether in environment or safety and health, or pricing, or labor relations, or the comprehensiveness of business done by a single unit or in judging the social performance of a business unit, the corporate response to marketplace reactions has at least some chance of survival. This chance is denigrated with each turn of the governmental wheel of central direction.

Now new legislation is considered piecemeal by Congress with the pros and cons of each new law given a chance to be aired. But the new proposed standards would involve putting group managements under a stultifying inflexible commission-type of regulation with rigid guidelines that contrast sharply with the flexibility allowed in corporate initiatives over the last 200 years.

This bit of comment—or should I say, lament—on governmental embrace appeared in *The Wall Street Journal:*

GOVERNMENT REGULATION and red tape threaten to grow despite Ford's vows.

Energy officials ready a tough quiz for the oil industry, seeking to monitor all profit sources and outlays; executives fume that health officials refuse to abandon support of a bill regulating medical devices despite White House pressure. A special commission will surely propose new regulations to protect personal privacy.

Against industry objections, HEW Secretary Mathews adamantly upholds new rules designed to hold down prescription-drug costs. Transportation officials stick with tough auto-safety rules; truckers charge that a new brake requirement actually increases danger. A new law on disclosure of home buyers' closing costs breeds red tape; Congress moves to ease it.

But job-safety enforcers insist that they are trying to simplify regulations, make allowances for small business in imposing penalties.[3]

So the regulatory mill grinds on. We look at the past in order to learn from it. But it is not a useful exercise to try to relive 1900 or 1950 in 1975. The factors are new and different. We undoubtedly do have more regulations than we can use or deserve. Yet in a changing world, an energy-dependent world, with its massive increase in population, a well-documented need for some regulations exists. The question is how to regulate to best advantage.

THE LEGISLATIVE BALANCING ACT

The wise legislator must constantly do a balancing act. Will the legislation do more harm than good? Is it necessary to do it in a way which will hurt production? Is it advisable to throw even a small piece of the baby out with the newly proposed legislative wash water?

In the coal industry, for example, the accident rate varied widely under the old regulations which existed prior to 1972. Some operations, less alert to safety precautions, had ten times the accident rate of other operations in similar territory. Hence it could be concluded that some managements were not doing an adequate job.

A new law in 1972 and new regulations, however, swept away much that was good along with the inadequate. Safety inspectors swarmed into the mines. The costs of operation went skyhigh and productivity dropped as much as 20 to 30 percent.

Granting for this purpose some changes were advisable, were the changes that were selected the best possible, all things considered? Personally, I have great sympathy with miners and concern for their working conditions and especially their safety. "Safety first" should mean what it says. But an improvement in working place requirements need not be a monstrosity from the standpoint of productivity. The change in this case illustrates how an act of regulation creates an unnecessary economic load and transfers that load from the mine site to the public generally for that is where lower productivity sooner or later shows up in higher costs and higher prices. It also indicates the delicate balancing act the legislator is constantly called upon to perform and how important his qualifications are for the job of legislating.

In a way, business units are caught in a supply-consumption pull and haul. Many of us, without too much regard for supply, are engaged in dividing consumption more equitably, as we see it. Not being in the supply end we assume it will take care of itself since it generally has. Or we reason the more equitable division will somehow help supply. Or for those of us who are born regulators there is nothing we would rather do than regulate for the sake of regulating. It is a form of self-satisfying preoccupation.

In discussing the benefits of flexibility for business units I am in reality searching for a method of preserving some opportunities for the supply side. I have the old-fashioned notion that more opportunity for flexible operation will result in more and better bread being baked and that if more rather than less bread is baked everyone in the family will benefit. Saying it another way, if at least some freedom and some opportunity for exercising ingenuity is retained for the business unit, we will all be benefited.

Now, of course, that does not seem to help the hapless autoworker who is out of work with his many weeks of supplemental unemployment benefits about exhausted. Perhaps not immediately nor in the full amount he would need or desire, but less regulation on the supply side helps his supply of a job or of food. It is not the perfect way, perhaps, but it is the best way yet devised to give that worker an economic chance.

NATIONAL ECONOMIC PLANNING

Like Federal standards or Federal incorporation, economic planning for the United States is not a new subject. Until recent months it had its greatest impetus in the thirties. Perhaps a few will recall the National Recovery Act which was born in 1933 and lived until 1935 when it was found unconstitutional by the Supreme Court. The Bituminous Coal Conservation Act and the Agricultural Adjustment Act were, in a sense, a form of national planning and were also found to be unconstitutional. President Roosevelt followed his legislative frustrations with an all-out attempt to pack, as it was called, the Supreme Court in 1937, but that was unsuccessful. The Temporary National Economic Committee was created in the late thirties and was headed by Senator Joseph C. O'Mahoney. It produced little.

In passing, it may be said that with all the new laws and efforts at Federal economic involvement in the thirties, nine years after the Depression began, the unemployment rate, while not at its height, reached about 19 percent in 1938.

The composition of the Supreme Court has changed, and, although it is still interpreting the same constitution, the circumstances keep changing and some forms of national planning are likely to have a different reception than in earlier years.

The most recently organized example of pushing forward with national planning is sponsored by a group of economists, labor leaders, and businessmen led by Wassily Leontieff until recently of the Harvard faculty and now at New York University.

This group seems to share a conviction that if the economic life of the nation is to be improved, systematic attention must be given to the future. They believe that national planning must be made respectable in a democracy and the machinery for planning established. They suggest an office of national economic planning in the Executive Branch of the Federal Government to operate in partnership with a joint congressional planning committee.

Broadly, the purposes would include collection from all public and private sources of much more detailed economic information. Long-range plans would then be determined for the country. If adopted, they would serve as guidelines for business, labor, and the populace generally. Coordination of administrative governmental activities are also said to be required.

Can a nation thrive on national planning? Is it the wave of the future? Can it properly be compared with corporate planning with which every corporate manager is daily involved?[4]

It can be said on the affirmative side that Congress has enacted a number of so-called plans for various segments of national activity over the years, for example, an agriculture plan, and a plan for housing, and a plan for shipping, and one for rail transportation, and for imports and exports, and for watching money supplies through the Federal Reserve.

Interestingly enough, little attention seems to be paid currently to the effect of national planning on antitrust theories. The Sherman Antitrust Act enacted in 1890, the Federal Trade Commission Act and the Clayton Act in 1914, as well as the common law, were foundation pieces of competitive or antitrust policy.

This antitrust policy presumes that it is economically healthy for the nation if each business unit would reach its own individual conclusion with respect to what it will make, where it will make it, what fields of competition it will enter, and the manner in which it will discharge its corporate responsibilities, all within the boundaries prescribed by statute and case law.

It is also true that there has been less than perfect competitive performance under antitrust laws by corporations. But, by and large, competition as a way of life has thrived, been enforced, and its operation has benefited the public. Over the years, better mouse traps have continually been built and marketed while less useful older design mouse traps have been forced to be discontinued. National planning in reality is the submergence of the competitive principle.

It is useless to protest against all instances of national planning. In emergencies we may well need, for example, some form of a nationwide energy program. If shortages of energy come again, as they may, fuel allocation is likely to occur which is a form of planning.

Yet that process of piece-by-piece planning with, hopefully, minimum controls, has advantages, I believe, over the broader form of national planning which will result sooner or later in rather rigid corporate directives. And it does not mean, for example, that Congress must restructure or virtually nationalize the oil industry or place the oil corporations under federal charter.

Moreover, it certainly has not been demonstrated to date that the regulatory agencies, such as we now have in many areas, have succeeded in providing by shining examples the rewards of national planning.

FAITH IN WASHINGTON PROBLEM SOLVING FALTERING

And let me hasten to say that faith in Washington problem solving is faltering, that prevailing types of regulation and its sheer volume is causing considerable doubt.

Lately there have come from the academic world serious proposals for removing barriers to market reactions in the competitive area. To this end it is suggested that restrictions on the movement of agricultural products between states, production quotas, and export subsidies be reexamined; that transportation routes and rates become less restricted and more competitive, and subsidies for shipping be abolished; that natural gas control at the well head be ended; that petroleum allocations and oil price controls be terminated; that banking freedoms relating to interest payments and areas of competition be enlarged; that resale price maintenance be ended; that the antitrust laws be revised; that merger guidelines be reformulated; that changes be made in labor laws relating to membership, apprenticeship, hiring halls, and government contracting; that limitations on imports be modernized; and that some government operations be made subject to competition.

Another criticism arises from governmental regulators themselves. Some months ago, for example, the Chairman of the Federal Trade Commission, Lewis A. Engman, said,

> What we were given to believe was that, if the nation had a problem, Washington would solve it. It was the common faith. The government was wise, the government was able, the government was just. . . . In time of trouble, what better place to turn. And so we turned.
>
> With quiet faith we consented as layer after layer of controls and regulations were superimposed on our free markets. When the desired results were not forthcoming, the prescription was for more of the same. . . . The resultant waste and inefficiency is all around us, some of it obvious in the form of higher prices, some of it hidden in the form of uneconomic resource allocation. . . . Obviously, in a democratic society with an economy as complex as ours, we may decide in the political process that there are some problems which are beyond the power of the market to correct, or which should be dealt with in spite of the market. But what I *am* suggesting is that if we do this, we should know the cost—it is past time for us to define what is "proper" and what is not, and to act accordingly.[5]

In November 1975, it was reported that "Labor Secretary John T. Dunlop had proposed that the Ford Administration make a subtle but fundamental change in the way the Government should develop and enforce regulations that affect the pocketbooks, health, and safety of millions of Amercians."[6] The article referred to a paper circulated within government and now made public that contained a proposal which had already, it is stated, "stirred considerable hostility."

According to this article, the proposal seems to be that the "key to improving the existing regulatory effort is to give the contending parties a larger role in writing regulations and deciding how that will be enforced." The draft proposal argued that the existing method for developing Federal regulations is "inherently contentious and acts to maximize antagonism between the parties." The Secretary of Labor is quoted as saying, "The rule-making and adjudicatory procedures do not include a mechanism for the development of mutual accommodation among conflicting interests." Also, that "The country needs to acquire a more realistic understanding of the limits to the degree to which social change can be brought about through legal compulsion."

GREAT BRITAIN TRIES HARDER

Great Britain is recognized as a leader in welfare programs, high taxes, nationalized industry, and what has been termed, "quasi-socialist orientation." However the press has reported a marked shift in emphasis: "Britain to Stress Industry in Shift of Economic Aims—Welfare Programs' Priority Reduced as Wilson Seeks High Output and Earnings—A Basic Policy Revision—Government Revokes, for at Least 5 Years, Strategies That Prevailed since '56."[7]

In a policy document Prime Minister Harold Wilson is quoted as saying, "For the immediate future, this will mean giving priority to industrial development over consumption or even our social objectives." He also indicated that government, industrial, and labor leaders have endorsed the program.

If true, this can only be characterized as an astonishing development. If this new British policy is to be given a chance to function, promptly and unequivocally the industrial organizations still existing in Great Britain must be "unfettered" much more than they have been. For anyone who has been steeped in the old system which existed for the past 30 years, it will be the most difficult kind of decentralized decision medicine to take. If Mr. Wilson's new policy succeeds, someone in Great Britain is entitled to a high accolade terming him the author of this century's regulatory miracle.

Leaving the example of Great Britain, I am not unaware of the interest on the part of some in our nation in national planning. It is a fertile field for generalizations and ideological speculation.[8] All of us have also noted the high degree of national planning in certain nations abroad. For those who believe the Marxist type of state planning may have advantages, I recommend a reading of Solzhenitsyn's *Letter to the Soviet Leaders*.[9] But one should also note the work of T. C. Koopmans who is the Alfred Cowles Professor of Economics at Yale and a co-winner of the 1975 Nobel Prize in Economic Science.[10]

A FINAL WORD

A review of 200 years in the economically productive life of our fruitful nation must necessarily be sparingly brief. Several points, however, can be made. One is that starting practically from scratch, groups of people organized into business units showed constant initiative and innovation; their efforts produced economic bounties the like of which have not before been available to man anywhere. It also is a reasonable conclusion that devising the privately financed, privately operated corporation as a means of assembling and concentrating the efforts of many people on single and multiple projects of their own choosing has been highly successful from a production and employment point of view.

It is likewise clear that along with creative group efforts we as a nation have erected a complex confining system of regulation which has grown to large dimensions. And it is destined to grow even larger. It is as though a strong vine were rising in the fruit tree and engulfing the tree's lifegiving branches almost to the point of strangulation.

For the future, as observed, it appears that still more regulations are to come; that during the next decades the major conflict to be hammered out in the economic field is the constant struggle between just enough regulation and too much regulation, between governmental controls of a detailed, specialized, and centralized nature, on the one hand, and the opportunity for decentralized production and decision making and managerial initiative, on the other.

It is hardly an answer to this problem to declaim, as some have, that our basic problem is ignorance of the facts and that when we do it piece by piece, it is really inept expediency which is doing the national planning. Such an analysis fails to focus attention on the undesirable effects on production of the intertwining vines of regulation. It fails to recognize the dependency of the entire productive machinery of this nation upon decentralized decision making.

Looking ahead, some national planning and some Federal standards will undoubtedly come to pass legislatively. Their content will be of the greatest importance and the theories motivating them of even greater importance.

The payload for the nation from group activity in the field of production during the coming decades will depend on the flexibility given it. That flexibility, that decentralized decision making, is the bread of life in the functioning of business units. Without it the good results our nation has had will be endangered.

In this bicentennial year, I urge only that we look at the past to learn more about the avenues to good fortune for the future. Spotty as our past has been, it is nevertheless quite credible. It can be a prologue to our future.

NOTES

1. *The Washington Embrace of Business,* 1974 Benjamin F. Fairless Memorial Lectures at Carnegie-Mellon University (New York: Columbia University Press, 1975), p. 18.
2. "Nader Group urges the Federal Chartering of Big Corporations," *The New York Times* (January 25, 1976), p. 28.
3. *The Wall Street Journal* (October 31, 1975), p. 1.
4. Henry C. Wallich, "No Talent for Planning," Annual Meeting American Economics Association, Dallas, Texas, December 29, 1975. Also, Robert L. Heilbroner, *New York Times Magazine* (January 25, 1976), p. 9.
5. Remarks at the Business Council meeting, Hot Springs, Virginia, May 10, 1975.
6. *The New York Times* (November 9, 1975), p. 1.

7. *The New York Times* (November 6, 1975), p. 1.

8. See, for example, George C. Lodge, *The New American Ideology* (New York: Alfred A. Knopf, 1975).

9. (New York: Harper & Row, Publishers, Inc., 1975.)

10. *The New York Times* (October 15, 1975).

FIVE

The Federal Reserve and the Failure of Franklin National Bank: A Case Study of Regulation

Andrew F. Brimmer

Thomas Henry Carroll Ford Foundation Visiting Professor
Graduate School of Business Administration
Harvard University

In the history of American banking, October 8, 1974, will stand as a date to be remembered. On that day, the Franklin National Bank failed. Nine months earlier, with total assets of $4,999 million, it had been the nation's twentieth largest bank. By the time it was declared insolvent, its total assets had shrunk to $3,646 million.

Having declared Franklin insolvent, the Comptroller of the Currency simultaneously appointed the Federal Deposit Insurance Corporation (FDIC) receiver of the bank.[1] The FDIC promptly accepted the highest among the four bids submitted earlier on October 8 for the assumption of all of Franklin's deposit liabilities (then in the neighborhood of $1,369 million) and the purchase of Franklin's assets of equal value (less the purchase bid price), including the right to choose among each of Franklin's 104 offices. The winning bid (of $125 million) was submitted by European-American Bank and Trust Company (European-American). This

FDIC-insured, New York State chartered, nonmember bank is owned jointly by six of the largest banks in Europe. It had combined assets of more than $90 billion in October, 1974.[2]

The Federal Reserve Bank of New York lent Franklin National Bank just over $1.7 billion during the final months of the bank's life. The FDIC assumed that liability. By December 31, 1975, the FDIC had repaid $598,475,000 from the collections arising from its administration of the receivership. There is no doubt that by the time the loan matures in 1977 (if not before), the FDIC will repay the Federal Reserve in full.

A great deal has been said about the role of the Federal Reserve and other Federal bank regulatory authorities in the failure of Franklin National Bank. The Federal Reserve in particular has received accolades as well as some criticism. On the one hand, the System is seen in some circles as having done a superb job in carrying out its role as a lender of last resort. However, some members of Congress, as well as a number of observers in the public at large, have suggested that the Federal Reserve wasted taxpayers' money by extending loans to an institution whose failure was inevitable.

I do not wish to join explicitly in this debate. Yet, there are aspects of the Federal Reserve role in this episode which ought to be illuminated further. These considerations extend beyond the traditional functions of the Federal Reserve as a lender of last resort for the banking system. Since Franklin—a member of the Federal Reserve System—could not obtain funds anywhere else during the final months of its troubled life, the Federal Reserve was the only alternative it had available. So the question is this: Why did the Federal Reserve permit the loan to Franklin to assume such enormous proportions, and why was it extended over such a long period? These questions take on even greater import when we realize that, as early as mid-June, 1974, members of the Federal Reserve Board, as well as senior officials in the United States Treasury Department, had accepted Franklin's failure as a high probability.

For an answer to these questions, one must look well beyond the simple conception of the Federal Reserve as a lender to member banks in distress. Instead, the central bank must be seen as having fundamental responsibility for the health and functioning of the financial system as a whole. Specifically, in financing Franklin's needs for the five months when the Federal Reserve knew that Franklin would ultimately fail, the System had its eyes on a range of considerations extending well beyond Franklin. These included a deep concern about the access of large regional banks to the nation's money markets. As Franklin's difficulties unfolded, an increasing number of these regional institutions found investors becoming more and more reluctant to accept their negotiable certificates of deposits (CD's). These investors in turn were reacting to the sharply increased perception of risk that had been generated by the failure of several large banks in this country and in Europe. Moreover, the progressively deteriorating situation of real estate investment trusts was also a negative factor. Consequently, one of the principal aims of the Federal Reserve during the summer of 1974 was to minimize attrition in the CD segment of the national money market.

Another objective was to minimize the danger to the international money market which would have been heightened by an early collapse of Franklin National Bank. On the eve of its failure, Franklin National had about one-fifth of its total liabilities on the books of its London branch. As Franklin's difficulties progressed, the London branch lost a substantial fraction of its Euro-dollar deposits. So, a sizable proportion of the Federal Reserve's loan to Franklin was used to cover attrition at the London branch. Moreover, the Federal Reserve Bank of New York, just prior to Franklin's failure, acquired the latter's foreign-exchange commitments of $725 million. This was done to relieve the uncertainty both here and abroad created by the overhang of such a large volume of liabilities. Both of these developments represent an extension of central bank responsibilities beyond the boundaries traditionally conceived.

Since my resignation as a Member of the Federal Reserve Board did not become effective until August 31, 1974, I participated in virtually all of the major decisions which shaped the Federal Reserve's strategy in its handling of the Franklin situation. It is mainly on that experience that I have drawn in the following analysis. First the rise and fall of Franklin National Bank is described. A brief sketch is provided of Franklin's growth and expansion from a fairly prosperous retail banking organization on Long Island into wholesale banking in New York City and on into international banking in London. In the next section, the roots of the Franklin Bank failure are discussed. In particular, the crucial impact on Franklin's fortunes of the Federal Reserve's decision to deny Franklin

National New York Corporation's acquisition of Talcott National is explained. Finally, the money market focus and strategy in the Federal Reserve as it sought to cope with the Franklin situation are explained and appraised.

RISE AND FALL OF FRANKLIN NATIONAL BANK

To appreciate the environment in which the Federal Reserve and other regulatory agencies had to cope with the Franklin situation, it is necessary to have at least a rudimentary understanding of the evolution of Franklin National Bank as an institution.[3] By mid-1974, Franklin was really three institutions: (1) a fairly strong retail bank with a wide branch network based on Long Island; (2) a wholesale bank which for ten years had been struggling (without much success) to make its way in the highly competitive environment of New York City, and (3) a small international banking institution recently arrived on the foreign scene with few secure international customers. We can look briefly at each of these conceptually separate institutions living comfortably in one (not well-managed) house.

Growth and Expansion of Franklin

In April, 1934, Arthur Roth arrived in Franklin Square in Nassau County on Long Island to take over a small institution left stranded by the Great Depression. The bank's balance sheet showed total deposits of $478,000 and total capital of $125,000. However, according to Roth, the depreciation in the bank's bond portfolio amounted to $200,000. Losses in the loan portfolio (not written off) were about $50,000. The bank had four employees, and it was located in a community with a population of 3500.

The first task facing Roth was the refinancing of the bank. To this end, he appealed to the Reconstruction Finance Corporation (RFC) for assistance. The RFC advanced $100,000, taking as security $50,000 (face value) of Franklin National preferred stock plus a $50,000 capital note guaranteed by the bank's Directors (several of whom had to use their own homes as security). Partly with the proceeds of this transaction, Roth wrote off $50,000 of losses in the loan portfolio, and the bank's capital was scaled down to $50,000. Thus, Arthur Roth and Franklin National Bank started off in the spring of 1934 with a clean bank.

From the very beginning, Roth based his plans for Franklin National squarely on the future of Long Island and especially on Nassau County. But at that time, there was little demand for business loans which were the traditional backbone of the typical bank. However, home building in Nassau County—partly because of the stimulative impact of Federal Government programs—was beginning to stir. Roth's father and brother were both builders. In fact, he had frequently done accounting work for them, and this had taught him something about the housing finance business. Through other contacts on Long Island, he began to provide construction loans for home builders and later undertook to provide mortgage money for home buyers, as well. Since Franklin National's deposit base could not support retention of these mortgages, it was necessary to place the mortgages with long-term lenders. Getting little or no response from New York City institutions, Roth sought—and got—accommodation at several New England life insurance companies. With these institutions as anchor, he was subsequently able to broaden his outlets to include savings bank in New England and still later in Brooklyn, as well. Ultimately, some of the bigger commercial banks on Long Island became willing to take the mortgages.

So, the expanding market for housing on Long Island became one of the mainsprings of Franklin's growth. In addition, Roth promoted the growth of industry in Nassau County. His principal aim was to provide alternatives to commuting to jobs in New York City and to enhance the generation of income (and banking) opportunities in the county. These efforts were followed by a campaign by Roth to obtain for his bank the legal right to use the word "savings" in advertising for consumer time deposits. The case went all the way to the Supreme Court of the United States, and Roth won.

Parallelling these efforts was a vigorous drive on the part of Franklin National Bank to create a strong retail branch network in Long Island. This campaign was immensely successful. By December 31, 1973, Franklin had 49 branches in Nassau County and 24 in Suffolk. Its remaining 31 branches were in New York City. So, almost half of Franklin's 104 branches were in its home county where it had gotten started. Just under one-quarter was in Suffolk County, and 30 percent were in New York City. More importantly, although the large Manhattan-based banks and bank holding companies have made headway in Long Island in recent years, Franklin was still holding its traditional ground at the end of 1973. In competition with this group, Franklin still had one-third of the combined offices in Nassau and one-quarter of those in Suffolk County. In sharp contrast, it had only 4 percent of the branches in New York City.

As of June 30, 1973, Franklin National held $2.5 billion of deposits. About $853 million of this amount (just over one-third of the total) were held in Nassau County, and another $315 million (13 percent) were held at the Suffolk branches. The remaining $1.4 billion (55 percent) were held at New York City branches. On the same date, these New York City branches accounted for only 1.8 percent of the total deposit held by the ten bank holding companies. In contrast, Franklin still had 50 percent of the deposits held by the group in Nassau County and 37 percent of their holdings in Suffolk County. So, despite its move into New York in the mid-1960's, Franklin remained a bank whose activities were deeply rooted in the economy of Long Island.

Wholesale Banking

The move into New York City in 1964 was made possible when the Comptroller of the Currency finally authorized a branch for Franklin after numerous applications had been turned down.[4] This entry put Franklin into direct competition with the giant New York institutions not only for retail business but, above all, for wholesale accounts. As a newcomer to the wholesale scene, Franklin naturally found it difficult to attract the best customers. In the process, it undoubtedly ended up looking for business among firms whose credit standing was for the most part below that of the other large banks competing in the wholesale field. But it is also clear that Franklin went well beyond this understandable tilting to attract borrowers. Undoubtedly, Franklin ended up making loans to many companies which previously had been accommodated primarily by factors and other nonbank commercial lenders. More fundamentally, Franklin extended such loans at interest rates at or only slightly above the prime rate which other banks were charging their best customers. In many instances, Franklin also required lower compensating balance ratios than those prevailing at other banks.

This greater willingness to take risks—and to do so on the basis of more liberal terms—enabled Franklin to register one of the fastest growth rates among all New York banks from the mid-1960s through the end of the decade. To finance this rapidly expanding volume of business, Franklin was an aggressive seller of CD's especially to regional banks and middle-sized corporations throughout the country. It also bid aggressively and persistently as a net purchaser of funds in the Federal funds market.

Table 1
Franklin National Bank

Net Income and Rates of Return, 1970-1973

	Franklin National		Large Banks in New York State
Year	Net Income (Millions)	Net Income as Percent of Total Assets	Net Income as Percent of Total Assets
1970	$22.9	0.66%	0.98%
1971	16.1	0.46	0.84
1972	14.2	0.33	0.78
1973	13.8	0.30	NA

NA: not available.
Source: Federal Reserve Board.

The impact of this growth strategy on Franklin's performance was generally negative. This can be seen in its net earnings and in the quality of its loan portfolio, (see Table 1). The rate of return on Franklin's assets during the three or four years prior to its demise was consistently below that achieved by other large banks in New York State. Between 1970 and 1973, Franklin's net income fell steadily— from $22.9 million in the earlier year to $13.8 million in its final full year of existence. Net income as a percentage of total assets shrank from 0.66 percent to 0.30 percent over the same period. The rates of return for other large banks in New York were also declining over the same interval, but the decrease was less sharp. Consequently, while

Franklin's rate of return was two-thirds that achieved by other large banks in 1970, the fraction had dropped to just over two-fifths in 1973.

The deteriorating trend in Franklin's loan porfolio is shown much more directly in the figures in Table 2.

Table 2
Quality of Franklin National Bank's Loan Portfolio, 1972-1974
(Amounts in Millions of Dollars)

Category	December, 1972		December, 1973		June, 1974	
	Amount	Percent	Amount	Percent	Amount	Percent
Not Classified	1,627.9	89.4	1,880.9	86.6	1,742.6	87.3
Classified						
Loss	7.0	0.4	12.0	0.5	13.5	0.7
Doubtful	22.0	1.2	40.0	1.8	40.0	2.0
Substandard	80.0	4.4	90.0	4.1	100.0	5.0
Special Mention	84.0	4.6	149.0	6.9	100.0	5.0
Subtotal	193.0	10.6	291.0	13.3	253.5	12.7
Total Loans	1,820.9	100.0	2,171.9	100.0	1,996.1	100.0
Memo:						
Equity Capital	162.6	—	167.8	—	142.9	—
Classified Loans as Percent of Equity Capital	118.7		173.4		177.4	

These data show the "quality" of Franklin's loans as judged by the national bank examiners during the examinations conducted in late 1972, late 1973, and mid-1974. The data on total loans outstanding are from the Call Reports which Franklin (along with all other insured banks) must fill out four times each year. The classifications used by the bank examiners are by no means precise, but by long-standing usage, they have come to be taken as general indications of the degree of risk of loss embedded in a loan porfolio at a given point in time. For a loan to be "classified," the examiner must feel after he has made an assessment of the circumstances and prospects for the borrower that the likelihood of the bank being repaid is somewhat less than that applying to the portfolio as a whole.

Four classifications are used: (1) loss; (2) doubtful; (3) substandard; and (4) special mention. Loans put in the loss category are those which in the examiner's judgement have no chance whatsoever of being repaid. As a rule, these losses have been charged against the bank's capital with little or no delay. Loans classified in the doubtful category are those against which examiners urged banks to establish proportionately high reserves against loss. Loans classified as substandard are those involving unusual delinquencies and which in other ways might pose serious problems for the bank. Loans in the special mention category are placed there as an early warning to the bank. Thus, categories (1) and (2) clearly pose the most serious difficulties, but the typical banker is also troubled by any significant expansion in the volume of loans placed in categories (3) and (4), as well.

The figures in the table show that, as of December, 1972, Franklin had total loans of $1.8 billion on its books. Classified loans totaled $193 million, representing 10.6 percent of the total. About $7 million was classed as loss, and $22 million of the loans were placed in the doubtful class. By the end of 1973, total loans had risen to $2.2 billion, but classified loans had climbed to $291 million representing over 13 percent of the total. Over the next six months, however, total loans declined by $175 million to $2.0 billion, and the volume of classified loans declined somewhat to $254 million or 12.7 percent. In the last six months of its life, Franklin's equity capital was also declining. Thus, a sharp runup occurred in classified loans as a percentage of equity capital.

In conclusion, Franklin's venture into the New York City money market and, above all, its attempt to prosper in the wholesale banking business was an extremely costly move for the bank. In a similar vein, its expansion into international banking turned out to be one of the principal factors in its downfall.

International Banking

Although Franklin had had an international department in its head office for a number of years, it made its major thrust into the international financial arena when it established its London branch in 1969. This made Franklin a part of the enormous expansion in the overseas activities of American banks which occurred in the mid- to late 1960s. In entering this arena, Franklin behaved essentially in the same way as did other modest-sized newcomers to the international scene: To build its volume, it was always ready to participate in many of the syndicated loans arranged through the interbank market centered in London. Many of those seeking funds in this market were marginal borrowers in terms of both risk and the degree of information which lenders had about them. While many were located in developing countries, still others were private firms in industrial countries which had heretofore found it difficult to get accommodation at traditional financial sources. Following the usual practice, Franklin charged such borrowers the prevailing London interbank rate (LIBO) plus a spread to cover risk and administrative expenses. However, Franklin—along with many other newcomer banks—became increasingly willing to shave the size of this spread in order to attract business. To finance its lending activities, Franklin was a vigorous bidder for funds (especially Euro-dollars) in the interbank market. Here, too, Franklin was frequently willing to offer potential depositors a premium above the deposit rate prevailing at the time.

To get a better understanding of Franklin's own experience, it might be helpful to pause briefly to sketch the main elements in the environment in which Franklin launched its major international banking effort.[5] One of the main objectives of many of the foreign branches opened after the mid-1960s was the provision of funds to their parents in the United States and especially during episodes of domestic credit restraint in 1966 and 1969-1970. These branches were also relied on to accumulate funds which could be rechanneled to other foreign offices in different parts of the world. Branches in the United Kingdom were especially active along these lines. But the largest proportion of the activities of the foreign branches was concentrated in the interbank market. This market consists of a network of foreign commercial banks with reciprocal arrangements for holding deposits and extending credits. At some point, of course, the individual banks participating in the interbank market would have to attract resources from beyond the boundaries of the banking system. Banks in London lie at the heart of the interbank market, but its geographic scope is far broader than the United Kingdom. Entry to the market is relatively easy, and this permitted even fairly small banks to launch foreign branches which could quickly accumulate sizable footings on their balance sheets.

Some of the foreign branches have been able to conduct a moderate volume of business with foreign governments and other official institutions. Initially, most of this business was probably the result of contacts developed by the parent banks. However, a number of the branches were able to venture out on their own to arrange Euro-currency loans for foreign official bodies including an increasing parade of borrowers from developing countries.[6] Some of them also were able to attract official deposits.

Basically, the principal motivation behind the opening of foreign branches by most of the banks in the United States which entered the field in the late 1960s and early 1970s was to meet the financial needs of their foreign customers—particularly multinational firms based in the United States. It will be recalled that regulations were promulgated in January, 1968, which limited the ability of American corporations to finance their foreign investment with funds from the United States. These regulations made it increasingly necessary for these corporations to borrow abroad. Under these circumstances, many banks in the United States essentially followed their customers overseas in an attempt to retain their business.

Franklin National Bank was squarely in the midst of this dash into international banking in 1969. By the end of 1973, it had accumulated about $1.0 billion of deposits at its London branch; it had outstanding roughly $600 million of loans, and the remaining $400 million had been placed (at interest) with other institutions in the interbank market. Thus, approximately one-fifth of its total business was focused in the Euro-dollar market. This fact assumed enormous importance in the Federal Reserve Board's efforts to cope with the host of problems generated by Franklin's floundering during the summer of 1974.

Profitability of Foreign Branches

In the meantime, the increasingly competitive environment prevailing in the international money and capital markets led to an appreciable narrowing of the spreads between lending and borrowing rates. For example, in early January, 1974, it was reported that prime borrowers in the Euro-dollar market could obtain loans at a cost of only three-eighths of 1 percent over the six-month interbank offering rate for deposits (LIBO). A year earlier, it was reported that many prime borrowers could obtain loans at rates in the neighborhood of five-eighths to three-quarters of 1 percent above the basic cost of money to the lenders. Moreover, it is quite evident that borrowers of less-than-prime standing also achieved accommodations at interest rates involving margins much more narrow than what could be gotten in late 1969 and early 1970 when other than prime borrowers were typically quoted rates ranging to 2.5 percent and more above the six-month Euro-dollar rate. This situation changed radically during 1973, and toward the close of that year, numerous borrowers, including many from less-developed countries previously not accorded a prime rating, were able to obtain funds on which the rate spread was set as low as five-eighths of 1 percent. In addition, maturities of the loans lengthened considerably—from a range of five to eight years in 1970 to as long as 15 years in late 1973.

It is very difficult to assess with any precision the way in which these trends have actually affected the profitability of the foreign branches of banks of the United States. Nevertheless, in the spring of 1973, I did make very rough calculations showing in broad magnitude the rates of return on the assets held by branches of American banks in London.[7] In January 1974, I made another and much more comprehensive effort to estimate the profitability of the foreign branches of the commercial banks of the United States.[8] For this purpose, information submitted to Federal bank supervisory agencies on the Call Report and in the statement of income was employed. Rates of return were calculated for the banks' domestic and foreign activities separately.[9] Complete reports were available for 64 banks covering the years 1969 and 1972. The banks were classified according to the following criteria: (1) banks with branches in a number of countries, that is, branches in two or more foreign countries; these were divided on the basis of their having established these branches before or after 1969. There were eight banks in each of these groups; (2) banks with London branches only.[10] In this group, there were also 16 banks. Eight banks had established branches before 1969 and eight afterwards; (3) Nassau branches only. There were 32 banks in this group all of which had opened branches since 1969. In addition, statistical information was obtained for 14 banks (included in categories 1 and 2 above) which show on a consolidated basis their foreign and domestic activities. These data were also used to estimate rates of return for these banks' total business. Finally, rates of return were calculated for all insured commercial banks in the United States; for all member banks of the Federal Reserve System, and for member banks with total deposits of $100 to $500 million and for those with deposits of $500 million and over.

The results are summarized in Table 3. Several facts stand out in these data. It is quite evident that, as a general rule, the profitability of the foreign branches of banks based in the United States was well below that experienced on their domestic business. The extremely thin rates of return achieved in the London market are even more striking. However, banks with branch networks in a number of countries were able to achieve a degree of profitability on their foreign business substantially above that achieved by banks that have restricted foreign activity to the London market.

More specifically, it should be noted that in both 1969 and 1972, banks which had only London branches were earning on the total assets of those branches a rate of return that was only one-quarter to one-third as large as the rate of return achieved in their domestic business. In contrast, those banks with a much more broadly based foreign network had a rate of return on branch assets in 1969 equal to just over half that recorded on their domestic assets. By 1972, however, they had substantially improved the profitability of their foreign branches—on whose assets the rate of return exceeded that obtained in their home market.

But, again, the adverse effect of the increasingly competitive international market is evident in the profits experience of those banks which developed their networks in a number of countries after 1969. In this case, the rate of return at their foreign branches in 1972 was only half that registered in their domestic business. In the case of Nassau branches, the rate of return in 1972 was over four-fifths as high as that achieved on the bank's domestic business. Of course, this is not surprising since the Nassau shell branches are little more than bookkeeping extensions of their head offices.

Finally, the profitability of the foreign activities of banks based in the United States can be compared with the profitability of banks in the United States as a whole. It will be noted that the yield on the assets of all insured commercial banks—as well as the yields on the

Table 3
Rates of Return on Domestic and Foreign Activities
of U. S. Commercial Banks, by Location of
Foreign Branches, 1969 and 1972

Class of Bank and Location of Branches	Rate of Return (Percent)			
	Domestic		Foreign	
	1969	*1972*	*1969*	*1972*
(1) Multi-country branches				
Established before 1969	0.69	0.57	0.37	0.63
Established after 1969	—	0.49	—	0.25
(2) London branch only				
Established before 1969	0.79	0.73	0.22	0.18
Established after 1969	—	0.63	—	0.22
(3) Nassau branch only	—	0.77	—	0.64

Memorandum:	*1969*	*1972*
All insured commercial banks	0.88	0.82
All Federal Reserve Member banks	0.85	0.80
with deposits of $100-500 million	0.92	0.77
with deposits of $500 million and over	0.80	0.71
Banks (14) reporting consolidated		
foreign and domestic activities	0.63	0.57

Source: Federal Reserve Board

assets of Federal Reserve member banks—were well above the rates of return estimated on the assets held by foreign branches of American banks. Moreover, the banks engaged in international activity generally reported rates of return below those for the American banking system as a whole. This was true even when the comparison was made with all large banks, represented here by Federal Reserve member banks with total deposits of $500 million or over.

From the foregoing review, it is quite evident that the increased competition in international money and capital markets had a significantly adverse impact on the profit margins of American banks operating foreign branches. Nevertheless, most American banks still found their overall experience in international financial operations sufficiently satisfactory as to justify remaining in the business.

ROOTS OF A BANK FAILURE

The foregoing account left us with the following picture of Franklin National Bank on the eve of its sudden descent toward bankruptcy: Its 73 branches in Long Island made it the strongest competitive force in retail banking in that segment of the New York metropolitan area. Its thrust into wholesale banking based in New York City had fallen short of the projected targets, and the entire effort was a serious drag on the bank's overall performance. Coming late to the international banking arena, Franklin was faced with a steep uphill climb to make its way against the strong—and risky— competitive gales blowing through the Euro-dollar market. In combination, these circumstances would have posed serious obstacles for Franklin National Bank and its management in the years ahead.

But these fundamental economic troubles were eclipsed in the late winter and early spring of 1974 by a convergence of developments which made the prospects for Franklin's survival extremely uncertain. These included the public revelation of sizable losses in the foreign-exchange market (some of which was due to fraud), as well as large losses resulting from speculation in United States Government securities. But the single most important factor which outweighed all of these was a decision by the Federal Reserve Board on May 1, 1974, denying Franklin New York Corporation's (the parent of Franklin National Bank) application to acquire Talcott National Corporation. In its public statement announcing the denial, the Board put a great deal of emphasis on the need of Franklin's management to devote its energies to the resolution of the bank's problems rather than attempting to extend its reach to encompass a large, diversified financial institution involved in factoring and other activities. However, in the background of this decision was an additional consideration that had troubled the Board for many months and which ultimately tipped the scales toward a denial. This concern centered on the role of Michele Sindona in the affairs of Franklin National Bank and its holding company. Each of these factors are considered briefly below:

Federal Reserve's Talcott Decision

The Board's decision to deny Franklin's acquisition of Talcott had its roots in an event that occurred almost two years earlier when Fasco International (Fasco) purchased one million shares of the outstanding common stock of Franklin National New York Corporation (Franklin Corp.) which was the bank holding company that was the parent of Franklin National Bank. Fasco, in turn, was a Luxembourg corporation wholly owned by Michele Sindona. This purchase, which cost Sindona $40 million, gave him ownership of 21.6 percent of Franklin Corp.'s outstanding stock and made him the largest single shareholder. Since Franklin Corp. owned 100 percent of the shares of Franklin National Bank, this meant that Sindona was automatically the largest single shareholder in the underlying bank subsidiary.

However, the exact legal status of Sindona with respect to Franklin National Bank was by no means clear. The key issue was this: Did Fasco exercise control over Franklin Corp.? If the answer were yes, under the 1970 amendments to the Bank Holding Company Act, Fasco had become a bank holding company—and thus obligated to get the Federal Reserve Board's permission to retain its stock ownership. However, this question was never explicitly answered on its merits. Instead, the Board's denial of the application by Franklin Corp. to acquire Talcott made the entire matter moot.

However, within the Federal Reserve System, opinions were mixed with respect to Sindona's legal status. On July 19, 1972 (barely a week after Sindona made his investment in Franklin Corp.), Congressman Patman wrote to the Federal Reserve Board expressing concern over Fasco's acquisition of such a large block of the stock of Franklin Corp. and asked what specific steps the Board intended to take regarding the matter. In response to this inquiry, in a letter dated August 2, 1972, Chairman Burns told Mr. Patman that the question of "control" of Franklin Corp. by Fasco could not be decided so easily. Instead, an investigation into the matter was promised.

While that inquiry was continuing, on March 29, 1973, the press reported that Fasco International had acquired 1.1 million shares (37 percent) of Talcott National Corporation's common stock—with the intention to acquire more than 50 percent of the total outstanding. Almost simultaneously (March 31, 1973), major changes occurred in the Board of Directors of Franklin Corp. and of Franklin National Bank. For some officials within the Federal Reserve, these actions put into sharp focus again the question of whether Sindona now had a controlling influence in the affairs of these institutions. However, in early April of that year, the Federal Reserve learned that the Regional Comptroller of the Currency in his periodic examination of Franklin National Bank (which ended in early March) had noted that the influence of Sindona was an "unknown factor" at that time. On April 6, 1973, the New York Federal Reserve was told by letter that, as of that date, Fasco International had acquired 1,600,000 shares of common stock of Talcott for $27 million. The money to purchase the shares had been lent to Fasco International by Fasco A.G. The schedule filed with the Securities and Exchange Commission in connection with the transaction said that the purpose of the acquisition by Fasco International was to make the shares available to Franklin Corp. It was also stated that the shares would be offered to the latter at cost. Finally, it was stated that Sindona intended not to make any recommendation to Franklin Corp. and that he would not vote when the matter came before the latter's Board of Directors.

On the basis of this information, by mid-May 1973, a number of officers within the Federal Reserve System had concluded that Fasco International and Fasco A.G. did, in fact, exercise a controlling influence over the affairs of Franklin Corp. Thus, in their view, both of these institutions had become bank holding companies and were subject to the Federal Reserve Board's jurisdiction.

But, on August 13, 1973, before that position could be presented to the Board for resolution, Franklin Corp. filed an application under section 4(c)(8) of the Bank Holding Company Act to acquire the shares of Talcott National. Apparently in response to informal reactions to this application by Federal Reserve officials (below the Federal Reserve Board level), in October, 1973, Fasco A.G. spun off shares of Fasco International to Mr. Sindona. On January 17, 1974, Franklin Corp. submitted an amended proposal to acquire Talcott. It provided that Fasco would increase its ownership of Franklin Corp. to over 25 percent of the latter's shares. Thus, Fasco—which was 100 percent owned by Sindona—would have to file to become a bank holding company. Such an application was, in fact, filed, and this prompted the Board to schedule for decision Franklin Corp.'s application to acquire Talcott National. That application was turned down on May 1, 1974.[11]

In making this decision, the Board noted that "Talcott, with total assets of $724 million, ranked as the 17th largest financial company in the nation as of year-end 1972 and as the nation's 11th largest independent finance company based on total capital funds." The Board concluded that the management by Franklin Corp. of such a large enterprise would severely strain Franklin's managerial talent. The Board also found that:

> [Franklin National] Bank itself has experienced an earnings record in recent years below the industry average, and has recently made a substantial shift in management policies designed to improve performance significantly. As changes in the institution's internal structure and asset composition are pursued, it is the Board's view that the acquisition of Talcott would be a complicating and diversionary factor. As the Board has previously stated on a number of occasions, a bank holding company should be a source of financial and managerial strength for its subsidiary bank. The Board finds that this proposal may constitute an undue claim on Applicant's managerial and financial resources and concludes that this represents an adverse effect to be considered under section 4(c)(8). . . .[12]

The above paragraph in the Board's statement denying the Franklin Corp. application to acquire Talcott alerted the entire public to what many participants in the financial markets—both here and abroad—already knew about the serious financial and managerial weakness inherent in Franklin's situation. The impact on Franklin was immediate. The attrition in deposits owned by sophisticated market participants, which had been evident for some time, accelerated noticeably. This market reaction was not a surprise to the

Federal Reserve Board. While the application was under consideration, the Federal Reserve Board staff explicitly called the possibility to the Board's attention. The Board, in turn, explicitly weighed the consequences of such a drain on Franklin's resources. Nevertheless, the Board also weighed the long-run effects—not only for Franklin but for the banking system as a whole—of permitting leading units in the nation's banking system to be controlled by a configuration of arrangements such as that inherent in the Sindona-Fasco-Franklin Corp. relationship. After careful deliberation, the Board concluded that such an outcome was against the public interest. Consequently, it denied the application.

MONEY MARKET FOCUS AND STRATEGY IN THE FEDERAL RESERVE

While market professionals read a great deal into the Board's May 1 decision and acted accordingly, the strongest spotlight was cast on Franklin National Bank on May 10, 1974, when it was announced publicly that the Bank's Directors had voted not to pay its customary quarterly dividend. The Bank also announced that, at its request, the Securities and Exchange Commission had suspended trading in shares of Franklin Corp. One of the reasons given was Franklin's need for more time to reevaluate and recalculate its first quarter earnings.

Earlier in the week (on May 7), Federal Reserve officials both in New York and in Washington, D. C., heard rumors to the effect that Franklin National Bank was bankrupt. Although checks were made promptly, the staff was not able to determine the source of the rumor. On the same day, however, officials of Franklin National Bank visited the Federal Reserve Bank of New York. The visit was motivated by their concern over the adverse effects which such a rumor would have on the availability of Federal funds to Franklin. In fact, they reported that a number of banks were already reluctant to supply funds to Franklin. As of that date, the Bank had actually suffered very little attrition, but they were afraid that the situation could worsen quickly. There was also a discussion of Franklin's probable need to borrow from the Federal Reserve Bank of New York. At the time, the

Franklin officers thought they might need to borrow about $150 million for three or four weeks.

During that meeting, Federal Reserve officials became aware of a problem relating to Franklin's London branch of which we were not aware when the Board acted on the application of Franklin Corp. to acquire Talcott. When the Board was considering that application, it was informed by the Board's staff that no special concern need be given to the $1.0 billion of assets and liabilities held in Franklin's London branch because these were structured on the basis of matching maturities. The Board's staff (along with the officials of the Federal Reserve Bank of New York) based its statements to the Board on assurances which they had received from the Office of the Comptroller of the Currency. Consequently, when the Board learned, on May 8, that no such matching maturities existed, the seriousness of the matter was recognized immediately. In fact, it appeared that roughly $600 million of funds in the London Branch had been acquired on a short-term basis (some of the money being held on a very short-term basis) and lent out on a medium-term basis. Consequently, if foreign sources of Euro-dollars were to dry up, the adverse effects on Franklin's operations would be enormous.

At this juncture, officials of the New York Federal Reserve Bank and the Board's staff made a decision which illustrates succinctly the central bank's concern with the money market implications of the difficulties evolving at Franklin National Bank. It was agreed that officials of the New York Federal Reserve Bank would ask the Regional Comptroller of the Currency (who had oversight responsibilities for Franklin's London branch, as well as for the parent bank itself) to station a resident examiner in Franklin National Bank. The staff also discussed the possibility of informing the Office of the Comptroller of the Currency in Washington that the Federal Reserve System—acting on its own initiative—would place a resident examiner in Franklin National Bank, if the Comptroller's Office were to decline to do so. The basis for the System's contemplated action was the prospect that the Federal Reserve most likely would have to lend a very large sum of money to Franklin National Bank.

That probability became a reality a few days later. With the passing of Franklin National's dividend on May 10, the Federal Reserve moved promptly to fulfill its traditional function as a lender of last resort. On Sunday, May 12, 1974, the Federal Reserve Board met in Washington. The Comptroller of the Currency and representatives of the Federal Depost Insurance Corporation (FDIC) also participated in the meeting. Simultaneously, officials of the Federal Reserve Bank of New York met, and they were also in direct contact with officials of Franklin National Bank. During the course of those meetings, it became clear that Franklin would have to borrow immediately an amount greatly in excess of the $150 million that its own officials had anticipated just a few days earlier. The Federal Reserve was prepared to provide such funds. So, at the conclusion of the meeting, it issued the following statement signalling publicly its intentions:

> Inquiries have been raised in recent days about the position of Franklin National Bank. The bank has reported a poor earnings record recently, and the management of the controlling holding company announced Friday that it would recommend that the regular dividend payment on both common and preferred stock be passed.
>
> The Board is familiar with this situation and looked carefully at the bank's condition in connection with the proposed acquisition of Talcott National Corporation by the bank's holding company. Its decision earlier this month was to turn down this proposal in part because it felt that management's energy should be devoted to the remedial program for the bank, which is now underway.
>
> There is, of course, the possibility that—with many rumors about the bank—Franklin National may experience some unusual liquidity pressures in the period ahead. As with all member banks, the Federal Reserve System stands prepared to advance funds to this bank as needed, within the limits of the collateral that can be supplied. Working with Franklin National, the Federal Reserve Bank of New York has determined that there is a large amount of acceptable collateral available to support advances to the bank from the Federal Reserve discount window, if they are needed.
>
> As a matter of general policy the Federal Reserve makes credit extensions to member banks, upon acceptable collateral, so long as the borrowing member bank is solvent. We are assured by the Comptroller of the Currency that Franklin National Bank is a solvent institution.

Table 4

Franklin National Bank, Source of Funds, 1974

	Amount ($ Millions) and Percent of Total Assets			
	May 3, 1974		July 31, 1974	
	Amount	Percent	Amount	Percent
Money Market CD's	$ 443	9.4	$ 107	2.8
Federal Funds (Net)	519	11.0	222	5.8
Repurchase Agreements	350	7.4	160	4.2
London Branch Deposits	926	19.6	394	10.3
Federal Reserve Borrowing	0	—	1,390	36.2
Subtotal	2,238	47.5	2,273	59.1
Other Sources	2,478	52.5	1,570	40.9
Total Assets	4,716	100.0	3,843	100.0

As the situation unfolded, Franklin National's borrowing from the Federal Reserve Bank of New York eventually reached a peak of $1.7 billion. Against this loan, the Federal Reserve Bank of New York held collateral with a value of about $2.0 billion. However, from the very beginning, Reserve Bank officials had a great deal of difficulty valuing the collateral, much of which consisted of loans extended by Franklin against the security of business inventories and a wide range of real estate and other types of property. Ultimately, the decision was made to accept the collateral on a fairly conservative discount basis—rather than attempting to arrange individual appraisals of the various items taken as collateral.

Deposit Attrition at Franklin National Bank

The sharp attrition in the bank's money market liabilities between May 3 and July 31, 1974 is shown in Table 4.

In early May, Franklin was financing almost half of its $4.7 billion of total assets in the domestic and international money market. It had obtained about 9.5 percent of its total resources in the domestic CD market, and about 18.5 percent had been acquired in the form of Federal funds. About one-fifth of the total resources was held at its London branch. By the end of July, Franklin's total assets had shrunk by about 20 percent, but its domestic and foreign money market resources had shrunk by 71 percent.

While Franklin also suffered attrition in its domestic demand deposits, as well as in time and savings accounts, the drain was far less dramatic. Demand deposits shrank by 35 percent and time and savings accounts by 32 percent. Franklin's total domestic loans declined by approximately one-quarter, and virtually all of this centered in commercial loans.

Thus, while Franklin was a floundering and steadily declining institution, it still needed access to some source of funds to replace the sharp attrition in deposits. In the end, the only source to which it could turn was the Federal Reserve System. But, as I have already indicated, in lending to Franklin, the Federal Reserve was also looking beyond that institution to assure the stability of the money market as a whole.

Growing Reliance on Purchased Money

The heavy dependence of Franklin National Bank on highly volatile short-term funds was simply a dramatic example of the basic revolution in commercial banking practices that had taken place over the previous decade. Increasingly, commercial banks had become willing to commit themselves to lend to their regular corporate customers—for which commitment the latter have shown a growing readiness to pay a fee. The banks, in turn, have made such commitments on the expectation that they could obtain funds as needed by bidding for Federal funds or by offering competitive rates on CD's. In other words, the banks have become increasingly prepared to buy resources to be rechanneled to their best customers.

The banks had come to rely on interest-bearing sources of funds prior to the failure of Franklin National Bank. The proportion of total resources on which the banks paid interest [13] was 32 percent in 1961; by 1971, it had risen to 50 percent, and by the end of 1973, it had climbed further to 55 percent.

The most significant change in the composition of these interest-bearing deposits was the dramatic rise in the volume of CD's. In 1961, the amount outstanding (while not reported separately) was known to be fairly small. By 1971, the volume had risen to $34 billion and accounted for 10.5 percent of the $320 billion of the banks' total interest-bearing liabilities. By December, 1973, the amount of CD's outstanding had increased to $64 billion—accounting for 14 percent of the total resources on which the banks were paying interest. The second significant change centered in the expansion of Federal funds purchased and securities sold under repurchase agreements. This category was not reported separately in 1961; but in 1971, such liabilities (primarily Federal funds) amounted to $24 billion—or 7.5 percent of all interest-bearing liabilities. In December, 1973, Federal funds amounted to $50 billion—representing 11 percent of total interest-bearing deposits.

Franklin National's Impact on the Money Markets

Against this background, Franklin National Bank and its problems appeared on center stage in the late spring and summer of 1974. Almost simultaneously (in June of that year), Bankhaus I. D. Herstatt, a private bank in West Germany, was declared bankrupt. A key factor in the bankruptcy was a large volume of foreign-exchange losses. In the third week of June, Franklin also stated publicly that it had lost $63.6 million during the first five months of 1974. About $46.8 million of Franklin's losses had also arisen from transactions in foreign exchange—most of which the bank said was unauthorized.[14] Several American banks also suffered losses because of the Herstatt failure. In combination, these events sent shock waves through both the domestic and international money markets. As uncertainties spread, depositors became extremely risk conscious and were more and more reluctant to deal with any bank except the handful of very large institutions whose stability appeared to be beyond question.

On the domestic scene, a handful of leading money center banks were beneficiaries of this search for safe havens. In contrast, a substantial number of large regional banks found it progressively more difficult to raise funds through offering their CD's in the national money market. Many of these banks depended substantially on the availability of such short-term resources to carry on their own business. The prospect that these banks would no longer have access to the national money market for a considerable time was one of the principal concerns motivating the Federal Reserve in its efforts to quarantine the adverse effects emanating from the Franklin situation. The extent to which commercial banks at the end of 1973 were

Table 5

Total Assets and Selected Money Market Liabilities
of Large Commercial Banks, December 31, 1973
(Amounts in Millions of Dollars)

CATEGORY	Total Assets	Purchased Money				Purchased Money as % of Total Assets			
		Euro-Dollar Borrowings	Federal Funds Purchased	Money Market CD's[1]	Total	Euro-Dollar Borrowings	Federal Funds Purchased	Money Market CD's	Total
I. *Money Center Banks*									
A. New York City (10 Banks)	177,627	715	10,785	26,892	38,392	0.4	6.1	15.1	21.6
B. Chicago (4 Banks)	38,483	490	4,194	9,166	13,850	1.3	10.9	23.8	36.0
C. California (7 Banks)	100,544	244	7,302	16,362	23,908	0.2	7.3	16.3	23.8
Sub-Total	316,654	1,449	22,281	52,420	76,150	0.4	7.0	16.6	24.0
II. *Regional Banks*									
A. Northeast (7 Banks)	33,160	33	2,703	4,188	6,924	0.1	8.2	12.6	20.9
B. Southeast (4 Banks)	11,472	0	1,199	1,699	2,898	0.0	10.5	14.8	25.3
C. Midwest (6 Banks)	20,626	2	1,736	2,223	3,961	0.0	8.4	10.8	19.2
D. Southwest (4 Banks)	14,031	0	2,336	2,104	4,440	0.0	16.6	15.0	31.6
E. West (4 Banks)	11,481	0	1,180	1,187	2,367	0.0	10.3	10.3	20.6
Sub-Total	90,770	35	9,154	11,401	20,590	–	10.1	12.6	22.7
III. Total (46 Banks)	407,424	1,484	31,435	63,821	96,740	0.3	7.7	15.7	23.7
IV. All Insured Commercial Banks (13,964 Banks)	827,081	1,502	50,410	64,391	116,303	0.2	6.1	7.8	14.1

[1] Negotiable certificates of deposit in denominations of $100,000 and over.

supporting their activities on the basis of money market liabilities can be seen in Table 5. These data show the banks' Euro-dollar borrowings, net Federal funds purchased, and money market CD's outstanding. Each of these sources is expressed as a percentage of the banks' total assets. The banks are grouped into several categories. Twenty-one banks in the money centers in New York, Chicago, and California constitute one group. Twenty-five large regional banks located in the Northeast, Southeast, Midwest, Southwest, and the Far West constitute the second group. These 46 banks in the two groups are among the 340 large banks which report weekly to the Federal Reserve. For comparison purposes, the same data are shown for the nearly 14,000 insured commercial banks at the end of 1973.

Several features stand out in these data. As one would expect, the large banks in the money centers were relatively more dependent on short-term liabilities than were those banks operating on a regional basis. The Chicago banks (with purchased money representing 36 percent of their total assets) were the most dependent among the several groups. However, several groups of regional banks (especially those in the Southeast and Southwest) also showed high liability-asset ratios. Among the different types of liabilities, money market CD's represented the largest fraction, but Federal funds were by no means insignificant.

Given the significant exposure of these regional banks to progressive attrition in their money market deposits, the Federal Reserve felt it was crucial that the adverse effects on them be cushioned. For this reason, several officials in the Federal Reserve thought it was important for Franklin National Bank to be seen as still having access to the money market aside from its borrowing at the Federal Reserve discount window. This was the motivation which led to significant Federal Reserve "encouragement" of the members of the New York Clearing House to participate in a pool of Federal funds made available to Franklin with a Federal Reserve guarantee. Under that arrangement, which was made effective in mid-June, 1974, Franklin was able to borrow a daily average of about $200 million of Federal funds which it otherwise could not have raised on the basis of its own standing in the financial markets.

Nevertheless, despite the Federal Reserve's efforts, many of the regional banks were not able to raise funds through the sale of CD's in the national money market during the summer and early fall of

1974. Instead, they reverted to reliance on investors in their own regions. Moreover, even after Franklin National had failed and the money markets had resumed much of their normal shape and function for a variety of reasons, many of these regional banks still did not have ready access to the national money market. In many cases, because, of their chilling experiences in 1974, some regional bankers still have not gotten up enough nerve to venture forth again into the national money centers.

Uncertainty and Deposit Behavior in the Euro-Dollar Market

As already indicated, Franklin's failure—combined with the bankruptcy of Herstatt—also had detrimental effects in the international capital markets. One of these effects was a sharp attrition in deposits at the foreign branches of American banks. This was especially true of interbank deposits at the foreign branches during the last half of 1974. The pattern of deposit flows leading up to and following the period of market uncertainty can be traced in the statistics published by the Federal Reserve Board. For example, liabilities to other foreign banks held by foreign branches of United States banks stood at $65.4 billion at the end of 1973—prior to the shock to market confidence resulting from the Herstatt failure and the public revelation of Franklin's difficulties. Again, it should be recalled that both banks (along with a number of others) suffered heavy losses because of speculation in the foreign-exchange market by some of their officers. Between December, 1973, and June, 1974, the branches' liabilities to foreign banks rose by $6.6 billion. Branches in the United Kingdom gained $1.7 billion and those in the Bahamas and Cayman Islands gained $2.4 billion—or 36 percent of the total rise. However, between June and December, 1974, the foreign branches of banks based in the United States taken as a group saw their liabilities to other foreign banks shrink by $6.3 billion. This drop was equal to 8.8 percent of the interbank liabilities on their books as of June, 1974. This large drop was offset by an increase of $6.5 billion in the branches' liabilities to foreign official institutions. Undoubtedly, a major part of the latter expansion is traceable to petroleum exporters. Other foreign depositors (mainly multinational corporations) reduced their deposits by $2.3 billion from June to December of 1974 although in the previous period they had raised their deposits in foreign branches of United States banks by $4.8 billion.

Among geographic areas, the attrition in deposits between June and December, 1974, was focused primarily in London, where the decrease amounted to $4.8 billion in the case of interbank deposits. For all liabilities of branches of banks based in the United States in the United Kingdom, the decline amounted to $1.5 billion. In the Bahamas and Cayman Islands, the attrition was about $2.4 billion in interbank deposits—while total deposits rose by $0.5 billion.

During the period of deposit shrinkage, loans to private borrowers on the books of foreign branches of United States banks rose by $4.8 billion. Claims on their parents rose by $0.4 billion and on other foreign branches by $2.6 billion. Claims on other borrowers rose by $0.8 billion. Consequently, the branches had to find other resources to sustain their lending. For the most part, they turned to their head offices and to other foreign branches of their parents.

But, in the case of Franklin National Bank, the parent of the London branch was in equally bad shape. Nevertheless, by July, 1974, the attrition in deposits at Franklin's London branch had forced the latter to rely on its parents for a net supply of $352 million. In contrast, as of May 3, 1974, the London branch had a small net surplus with Franklin's head office in London. But over the course of the summer, the total deposits of the London branch had shrunk from $926 million on May 3 to $394 million on July 31 of that year. Over the same period, however, the assets of Franklin's London branch declined much more moderately from $919 million to $746 million. Thus, the London branch had a shortfall of over $350 million which could be made up only from sources within the United States.

And there was only one such source, and that was the Federal Reserve. Between early May and the end of July, deposits at Franklin's London branch shrank by $532 million. Over the same time span, the assets of the branch declined by $173 million. So, Franklin's London branch had to find $359 million to support its operations. That money came from the Federal Reserve System.

As mentioned above, Federal Reserve officials learned as early as mid-May that Franklin's London branch was destined for trouble. After some debate (in which differences of opinion were never very wide) extending over several days, the Board agreed to interpose no objections to Franklin's use of borrowings from the Federal Reserve to

cover deposit attrition in London. To have done otherwise would
have hastened the collapse of the London branch perhaps even ahead
of Franklin itself. But more fundamentally, the Federal Reserve
recognized that a separate default at Franklin's London branch
would expose the entire Euro-dollar market to significant additional
dangers at a time when the international capital markets were
already suffering from excessive strains.

So, we can see growing out of the Franklin National episode
recognition by the Federal Reserve System of a new dimension in the
responsibilities of central banks. This was the clear and explicit
acceptance of the use of central bank resources to help stabilize
money markets beyond its own national boundaries.

CONCLUDING OBSERVATIONS:
LESSONS OF THE EXPERIENCE

From the foregoing experience, several lessons should be learned.
First, it is clear that the repercussions of the failure of Franklin
National Bank were quite different from those which attended bank
failures prior to the establishment of the Federal Reserve System, and
the experience is also in sharp contrast to that of the 1930s. The more
favorable outcome of the recent episode reflects both structural
changes in the banking system, as well as a considerably broader view
of its responsibilities taken by the Federal Reserve System. In
addition, the operations of the FDIC prevented large withdrawals
from other banks by frightened depositors, as happened in pre-FDIC
days.

In one sense, the difficulty which regional banks faced in trying to
market their CD's in the nation's money centers in 1974 reminds one
of the deposit management problems faced by regional banks under
the old National Banking System which prevailed prior to the
establishment of the Federal Reserve System in 1913. Under the older
system, so-called country banks in towns and smaller cities placed
their excess funds with banks in reserve cities when they were not
needed to meet local credit demands. This was typically the case
during the off season in agricultural areas. The reserve city banks in

turn shifted the excess funds to large banks in a few money centers—especially in New York and Chicago. As a rule, the banks in large money centers invested the funds in commercial paper, brokers' loans, and other highly liquid marketable financial assets. As the seasonal demand for funds expanded, these deposit flows were reversed. During periods of financial calm, this ebb and flow of funds to and from the central money markets worked well—and also provided local and regional banks with an opportunity to earn interest on funds which would otherwise be idle.

However, a rupture of the system at some point such as occurred during the financial panic of 1907 would lead to magnified repercussions throughout the banking system. Money center banks could no longer liquidate their short-term assets (without substantial capital losses) in order to meet the withdrawal of funds by regional banks. The latter, in turn, could not meet the claims of their country correspondents. Thus, local credit demands could not be met, and the adverse effects on real economic activity were extremely severe.

When the Federal Reserve System was started, one of its purposes was to overcome these deficiencies in the older banking system. However, the truly significant test came during the Depression of the 1930s, and the Federal Reserve failed in a spectacular way. Partly because of statutory limitations, but above all because of the Federal Reserve's narrow view of its own responsibility, the Federal Reserve was unable to act as a lender of last resort. As a result, thousands of banks with sound assets found that they could not maintain their liquidity in the face of the public's desire to withdraw deposits. Since the central bank was the only potential source of liquidity (which it failed to supply) a substantial fraction of the nation's commercial banks failed when they could have been saved.

Fortunately, in the Franklin National situation, the Federal Reserve did recognize its responsibilities to the nation's financial system. Through its efforts, it prevented the runoff of Federal funds and CD's at Franklin National from creating a flood of attrition at other banks around the nation, especially those which play a dominant role in various regions of the country. In the same vein, the Federal Reserve's willingness to permit the use of its funds to meet deposit attrition at Franklin's London branch undoubtedly helped to stabilize the Euro-dollar market.

The presence of FDIC insurance undoubtedly helped to sustain the confidence of smaller depositors at Franklin, as well as at other banks. As indicated above, while some attrition occurred in consumer-type deposits at Franklin, the runoff was much less proportionately than that which occurred with respect to CD's. There was virtually no decline in consumer-type deposits at other banks that could be traced to uncertainty on the part of small depositors because of Franklin's difficulties.

So, on balance, the Franklin National Bank case shows the nation's central bank and its deposit insurance institution cooperating to safeguard the banking system under conditions of considerable stress. Hopefully, the lesson taught by this experience will be learned—and remembered in the future.

NOTES

1. For a lucid exposition of the principal events leading up to the failure see Frank Wille, "The FDIC and Franklin National Bank: A Report to the Congress and all FDIC-Insured Banks," presented before the 81st Annual Convention of the Savings Banks Association of New York State, Boca Raton, Florida, November 23, 1974.

2. The details surrounding the transaction were extremely complicated and need not be examined here. In essence, as the successful bidder, European-American assumed the $1369 million of Franklin's deposit liabilities, as well as certain other designated balance sheet liabilities (amounting to roughly $266 million). European-American also had the right to select assets of Franklin in an amount which equalled the liabilities assumed, less European-American's bid price of $125 million. This net amount of Franklin's assets to be selected was subsequently determined to be $1490 million. As of December 31, 1975, European-American had selected all of the assets as required under the purchase and Assumption Agreement of October 8, 1974. European-American had also selected an additional $1,263,000 of assets for which it was scheduled to pay the receivership an amount equal to the present book value of such assets. As of the same date, European-American had specifically rejected all of Franklin's remaining assets except about $1,453,000 in fixed assets. Thus, through December 31, 1975, the FDIC had received for administration $2,153,227,000 of Franklin assets rejected by European-American in the selection process. In addition,

the FDIC was administering approximately $86 million in loans charged off by Franklin prior to its closing. So, the FDIC as receiver ended up with $2.2 billion (or 59 per cent) of the $3.7 billion of total assets which Franklin National Bank held at mid-year, 1974.

3. For a brief and entertaining account of the growth of Franklin National Bank, see Martin Mayer, *The Bankers* (New York: Weybright and Talley, 1974), pp. 92-97 and 114-116.

4. In passing, it should be noted that the granting of the application by James Saxon, who had been appointed Comptroller of the Currency by President John F. Kennedy, was over the opposition of the Federal Reserve Board. Even at that time, the Board felt that the maximum public benefits would derive from Franklin concentrating its efforts in the retail banking market of Long Island.

5. For a more comprehensive treatment of this general subject, see Andrew F. Brimmer and Frederick R. Dahl, "Growth of American International Banking: Implications for Public Policy," *The Journal of Finance* (May, 1975), pp. 341-363.

6. I discussed this subject in "International Capital Markets and the Financing of Economic Development," *Revenue de la Banque* (Belgium: 1974), No. 2.

7. See "American International Banking: Trends and Prospects," presented at the 51st Annual Meeting of the Bankers Association for Foreign Trade, Boca Raton, Florida, April 2, 1973, pp. 34-37.

8. "Prospects for Commercial Banks in International Money and Capital Markets: An American Perspective," presented at the Conference on World Banking organized by *The Financial Times,* London, England (January 17, 1974).

9. Some of the banks were operating abroad through wholly owned subsidiaries, and many of them also received income on minority investments in foreign financial institutions. However, this information was much more fragmentary, and it was not used in the calculations reported here.

10. In this classification as well as in the multicountry category were a few banks which also had Nassau branches. These Nassau branches were disregarded in this part of the analysis.

11. I did not vote on that decision since I was in South America on official Federal Reserve business. However, I had participated in most of the discussions leading up to the decision, and I also shared in the considerations of the Franklin matter until I resigned from the Federal Reserve Board effective August 21, 1974 within six weeks of Franklin's closure on October 8.

12. *Federal Reserve Bulletin* (June, 1974), p. 459.

13. These interest-bearing resources are defined here as total liabilities and capital minus demand deposits, bankers' acceptance outstanding, minority interests in consolidated subsidiaries, total reserves, and equity capital.

14. As matters developed, some of Franklin's foreign-exchange staff were indicted and charged with fraud.

SIX

THE EVOLVING ROLE OF ACCOUNTING

Michael Schiff

Vincent C. Ross Professor of Accounting
New York University

We can trace the history of accounting back more than 7000 years to the Chaldean-Babylonian, Assyrian, and Sumerian civilizations, along with specific references, such as "current money with the merchant," in the book of Genesis to Pacioli in the Middle Ages. But our interest in the evolution of accounting in the United States has a much shorter history and is limited to the twentieth century.

PRE-SEC YEARS

In the twentieth century, the center of accounting development moved to the United States, a consequence of the fulfillment of the American industrial potential.[1] The development of accounting standards during this period is typified by an interaction between government regulatory bodies and the profession, the latter going through a series of reorganizations in the process.

The first attempt at identifying standards for financial reports was made by the predecessor organization of the American Institute of Certified Public Accountants (AICPA), then called the American Association of Public Accountants. In 1909 it appointed a Special Committee on Terminology. Its report, resulting from six years of study, was adopted in 1915.[2] The creation of the Federal Reserve Board (FRB) and the Federal Trade Commission (FTC) by the Congress in 1913 and 1914 provided the vehicles for the first interactions between the public and private sectors in the development of accounting standards. The FRB promptly indicated a preference for commercial paper accompanied by certified statements and the FTC, within one year of its establishment, indicated an intent to establish a uniform accounting system for principal businesses possibly on an industry basis. Soon thereafter the FTC suggested a Federal register of accountants whose certificate would be acceptable to the FRB and the FTC. The profession's reaction was a hurried publication of a modification of a Price Waterhouse internal document on auditing which was revised in 1918 and entitled *Verification of Financial Statements.* This movement toward codification of some accounting standards was enough to satisfy the FRB and the FTC for the time being.

The aftermath of the sharp decline in market values in 1929 created new problems. The New York Stock Exchange, after extended meetings with the profession, ruled that all applications for listing must be accompanied by certified financial statements and, in 1933 the profession for its part designated a Special Committee on the Development of Accounting Principles whose charge was "to consider how far it may be possible to formulate broad principles of accounting which are regarded as so generally acceptable that any deviation from them should require explanation." [3]

The Congress was not impressed. For a while, it seriously considered the required audit of publicly held companies by accountants employed by the Federal government. It was only the earnest pleas of the profession and its assurances of its ability to do an adequate job that made the Congress forego this proposal. Instead, the Securities Act of 1933 vested in the FTC very broad powers over financial reporting, and in 1934 the Securities and Exchange Commission

(SEC) was created to carry out the objectives set forth in the Act. Congress opted to give authority on reporting criteria to a government agency, and thus to control auditors and those who prepare statements rather than employ Federal auditors to do the job.

It is worth noting that only one witness appeared in his capacity as an accountant before the Committee on Banking and Currency when it was considering the Securities Act. The accountant, Col. Carter, and Senator Gore agreed that some sort of a standard set of principles should be set up for each industry so that "Individual instances in each industry could be compared with each other." [4]

Former SEC Chairman Manuel Cohen observed that "the Securities Act when enacted did not require such uniform standards. Instead, the Commission was given probably the broadest grant of authority that it is possible for a legislature to entrust to an agency such as the Commission." [5]

1934 TO DATE

The period since 1934 has been typified by interactions between the SEC and the profession. On the one hand, the SEC has tried to exercise its legal option to remove the authority for setting accounting standards from the private sector, a threat periodically articulated by members of the SEC at different times and in different ways. In 1934 the commission stated, for example, that

> ... if we find that they [accountants] are unwilling or unable, perhaps, because of the influence of some of their clients, to do the job thoroughly, we won't hesitate to step in to the full extent of our statutory powers. [6]

On the other hand, the accounting profession, concerned with retaining the standard-setting role in the private sector and "under the gun" to satisfy the reporting objectives of the SEC, changed its structure to facilitate the development of standards.

Two aspects of the problem of evolving standards under the new conditions may be noted. First, the structure of the organization and second, the pursuit of a conceptual framework for accounting reporting to facilitate the setting of standards for both unresolved reporting problems of the past and emerging problems associated with changes in business organization and practices.

Institutional Structure

The profession's efforts to develop a viable structure have followed a pattern. When faced with a new set of problems or intense pressure from the SEC as well as internal and other external pressures, it has elected to reorganize. The trend predates the SEC. From the 1909 Special Committee on Terminology, reappointed and revitalized in 1920, to the Special Committee on Accounting Procedures, followed by the Accounting Principles Board (APB) to the current Financial Accounting Standards Board (FASB), the composition of these groups was dominated by practicing CPA's. Over time, nonprofessional accountants were added and indeed today, the members of the FASB serve full-time; the professional CPA's on the Board are completely severed from their firms. But they are addressing problems in pretty much the same way as others did in the past: identifying a problem and then seeking a standard which will be acceptable. In passing, it might be well to note that the process involves a series of steps, the key one being invitation of comments and public hearings before issuing a pronouncement; this is a process common to government administrative bodies and one used by the FASB's predecessor, the APB, from 1967 onward.

A critical commentator on the preoccupation with structure has cited the following purported observation by a Roman citizen in 60 A.D.:

> We tend to meet any new situation by reorganizing, and a wonderful new method it can be creating the illusion of progress while producing confusion, inefficiency and demoralization.[7]

One is tempted to suggest that procedurally, there has not been much change since that date.

Whatever the organizational structure of the profession, it had to work with the SEC. What characterized and continues to characterize this relationship is suggested by the SEC's Chief Accountant, J.C. Burton:

> In summary, the record indicates that the Commission and the accounting profession exist in a legitimate partnership for the protection of investors. Both have authority and responsibility.[8]

C. A. Lamden has observed that the notion of partnership is not as complete as is inferred above:

> The function of the SEC is to carry out the duties of a regulatory agency. There cannot be a partnership between regulators and those being regulated. They operate at different levels of authority.[9]

C. T. Horngren, a former member of the APB, viewed the partnership in another way:

> As I see it, SEC (top management) has used decentralization with a master's touch. Its lower level management (APB) does an enormous amount of work for no salary and has just enough freedom to want to continue the arrangement. Moreover, it is dominated by practitioners, the individuals responsible for the implementing the principles chosen. There is no evident efficiency here, because the work consists of both the formulation of principles and their implementation—an immensely complex task that will not be performed easily under any institutional arrangement.

He continues,

> . . . it is time to dispel the oft-heard myth that a private group is setting accounting principles which are then enforced by the policing agency, the SEC. The job of devising accounting principles is a joint effort, a private-public arrangement that should be explicitly admitted and publicized forthrightly by both partners along the top-lower management lines described here.[10]

The development of accounting standards relating to the invest-ment credit, purchase vs. pooling, and gains and losses on marketable securities would suggest that if the two organizations (SEC and APB) operated jointly, they were hardly equal partners. In fact, it has been suggested that:

> The fact that these two separate and distinct bodies are attempting to establish accounting principles is the primary reason, I believe, why we aren't solving our problems.[11]

Perhaps SEC Commissioner Sommer's statement in 1974 with regard to the newly created FASB summarizes the relationship:

> The extent to which the accounting profession has been permitted to create the rules under which it functions is not compelled by Congressional policy but, rather, a decision by the Commision, one which has been renewed now time after time for forty years, to allow the profession to exercise leadership.
>
> The decision is not a delegation of authority. It has been rather a willingness to permit the accounting profession to develop accounting principles and standards, always with the understanding that the final authority remained in the Commis-sion to determine whether the practices and principles adopted by the accounting profession and reflected in financial state-ments filed with the Commission were consistent with the Commission's conceptions of what was necessary for the protec-tion of investors.[12]

Framework for Accounting Principles

The profession's pursuit of a broad framework of accounting principles also suggests a pattern. From the *Statement of Accounting Principles* published in 1935 (a survey of practices and not really a statement of principles) to the 1952 *Reports of the Study Group on Business Income,* followed by *Accounting Research Studies 1* and *3* (1961-1962), to the *Report of the Study Group on the Objectives of Financial Statements* (The

Trueblood Study, 1973), the profession has had before it its own commissioned studies and has proceeded to ignore them. Much like its predecessors, at least to this point in time, the FASB is issuing pronouncements without such a framework.

Referring to the FASB's predecessor, the APB, J. C. Burton observed:

> The founders [of the APB] believed that research would make the best accounting answers apparent, that the function of the Board was essentially to anoint the truth that was determined through the efforts of many researchers in the accounting area. It didn't turn out that way, and, as a result, the Board had to turn to problem-solving as a method of achieving measurement principles which it was not really set up to do.[13]

From the profession itself came H.E. Kapnick's criticism:

> As a result of the failure to agree upon objectives, the Accounting Principles Board has gradually deteriorated over the years into an organization which issues more and more arbitrary and inconsistent rules rather than broadly based and logical standards or principles that are consistent with a set of guiding objectives. Each Opinion has been approached in an ad hoc manner, seeking to accommodate conflicting views with no clear expression of the goals to be achieved. Compromise has replaced principle and regulations have replaced reason. What a futile way to search for the lofty goals originally envisaged for the APB![14]

The fact that the attempt to set rules for accountancy is a futile exercise is not a recent bit of wisdom as Matheson noted in the British *Accountant* under the date *January 3, 1885:*

> ... (regarding) the absence from my book of exact rates of depreciation for different classes of plant, I am more on my ground, and I venture to assert that any positive statements of rates would be more likely to mislead than to inform ... fixed rules are impossible and examples, if offered for information, dangerous.[15]

The futility of rule making is underscored by J. Shank who observed: "No matter how detailed the rule, the mind of the enterprising entrepreneur will conceive a transaction consistent with the rule, and inconsistent with the spirit behind it." [16]

It is worth noting that the criticisms of the APB regarding its shift in emphasis to a rule-making body rarely mention the fact that the SEC induced the APB to do so. It was only with the publication of the Wheat Report in 1972 that specific references to the SEC's pressure on directing the APB toward its role as a rule-making body were made.[17] Interestingly enough, while the SEC encouraged the APB to write rules, J. C. Burton asserted in 1972 that "By writing precise rules, the Board made it possible for people to observe the letter and avoid the spirit with the blessing—and often assistance of their auditors." [18]

It is fair to say that the history of the FASB to date reflects to a significant degree a reaction to the determination of the SEC to develop rules with which to address specific accounting practices.

FULL DISCLOSURE

One important influence on the evolution of accounting in the United States has been a continuing pressure for full and complete disclosure in financial reports. This has been the basic thrust of the SEC, and, as a result, the American investor has been provided far more detailed financial information about the private sector and its components than his counterpart in any other democratic country. The latest amended rules of the SEC relating to annual reports requires that they contain at least certified statements for the last two years, a summary of operations for the last five years with managements' analysis of significant changes, a brief description of the company's business, a line of business breakdown, names and principal occupations of each director, and market price ranges and dividends paid per quarter during the last two years.

How much progress have we really made in disclosure? Perhaps we can see, if we look at the first annual report of U.S. Steel for the year ended December 31, 1902. While not typical of annual reports of that period, it does represent a level of disclosure which was decades ahead of its time. In form, it differs significantly in the absence of slick covers, graphs, charts, extended descriptive text, photos of products, and the smiling faces of officers and directors. The report did have 18 pages of pictures of *smoke-belching* plants of the company and three pages of typical ships and railroad cars owned by the company. The report provided:

A statement of accounting policy in the treatment of repairs and maintenance

Financial statements certified by Price Waterhouse

Production data—output in tons of some twenty products

Inventories valued at cost detailed for a total of 12 different product classifications

Bonded indebtedness—a full listing of all bonds outstanding for the company and its subsidiaries

Property Accounts—details of all capital expenditures classified by type of property acquired and by specific subsidiary and plant locations

Acquisitions—The purchase of a company is identified and the basis for acquisition

Orders on Hand—Unfilled orders on hand in quantity of product (tons) at the end of the current year and the last year

Summary of Financial Questions—A statement of uses and sources of funds almost identical to current summaries of financial statements. (This statement has been a required reporting standard only since 1971—APB No. 19)

Listing of All Plants—Seven pages of listing with details on types of mills at each plant

Quarterly Net Income—Quarterly data for the current year and the prior year. In addition *monthly* net income is supplied to permit determination of seasonal patterns.

Interestingly enough, when one contrasts the 1974 U.S. Steel Report with the one issued in 1902, the bulk of the notes in the 1974 Report deal with items which did not exist in the earlier year (employees' pension funding, stock option plans, tax litigation, etc.).

Another item which will improve our historical perspective on disclosure relates to the reporting of imputed interest in financial statements. Stephen A. Zeff indicates how this was reported in the 1900s. He noted that prior to the Institute's 1917 conventions, several prominent accountants were arguing for the inclusion of imputed interest as a cost of production. The issue came before the 1918 annual meeting and after a spirited discussion, was voted down, much to the dissatisfaction of a very vocal minority, a group which one year later, formed the National Association of Cost Accountants. The Institute responded by appointing a special committee to address the standardization of accounting procedures.[19]

Some 60 years later, in the fall of 1975, the FASB appointed a task force to study the accounting for interest costs; the scope of the project was to include a consideration of imputed interest on the cost of equity as well as interest on debt. Again the FASB was responding to a request by the SEC. ASR No. 163, issued by the SEC, declared a moratorium on adoption of the capitalization of interest by companies other than public utilities until such time as the FASB issues a pronouncement on the subject. The SEC noted that the increasing number of cases where interest was capitalized created a source of incomparability between financial statements of companies following different practices and hence the need for a position and guidelines.

A question can be posed at this point as follows: Given the evidence of the extent of disclosure some 70 years ago, admittedly not typical of reports of that period but indeed available, would we have progressed to where we are today without pressure from a government regulatory body like the SEC?

An empirical study of G. J. Benston concluded: ". . . the disclosure requirements of the Securities and Exchange Commission Act of 1934 had no measurable effect on the securities traded on the New York Stock Exchange." [20]

Benston's thesis has not received wide acceptance and questions have been raised about the relevance of his observations based on data for a period so different from that of the current economic scene. However, some writers have noted that investors generally either not care about the financial statements or cannot interpret them.[21]

In contrast to Benston's study, a recent survey of chartered financial analysts (400 were selected at random and 180 complete and usable replies were received) listed financial and other types of information normally used by analysts and requested the respondents to rate each information item for its importance in equity investment decisions on a scale of 5-1, from very important to very unimportant. Among items of high value (4.575 to 4.888) were earnings per share (in first position), amount of revenue and method used in its recognition, operating income for the period, accounting method (pooling vs. purchase), breakdown of sales, income and investment by divisions, product and lines of business, statement of changes in financial position, and so on. Many other items were listed, and it is interesting to note that price level adjusted financial statements as supplementary statements was listed as an unimportant item.[22]

W.H. Beaver urged that the FASB recognize the implications of research in finance theory in addressing its task. He observed:

> 1. Many reporting issues are capable of a simple disclosure solution and do not warrant an expenditure of FASB time and resources in attempting to resolve them.
> 2. The role of accounting data is to prevent superior returns accruing from inside information and can be achieved by a policy of much fuller disclosure than is currently required.
> 2. Financial statements should not be reduced to the level of understanding of the naive investor.
> 4. The FASB should strive for policies that will eliminate excessive costs of information.
> 5. The FASB should sponsor a full-scale research program in the areas indicated, so that it may have some evidence of the consequences of their choices among different sets of financial accounting standards.[23]

* * *

I should like to turn now to three issues concerning financial reports which are of importance and which might well serve to provide the bridge in this short review of the past, the present, and the future. The first deals with the problem of adjusting financial reports for the effects of price inflation, the second with international accounting standards, and the third with publication of earnings forecasts.

ACCOUNTING FOR INFLATION

The continuing price inflation since the end of World War II has resulted in considerable distortion in financial reports and has led to increasing concern with methods of handling this problem. One of the first attempts to deal with this problem was made by some steel companies to include an additional charge for depreciation beyond that based on historical cost in arriving at net income. This charge was treated as a deduction from after-tax income. The companies explained the additional charge as necessary to compensate for the effect of price-level changes on replacement costs. The reaction of the profession was to issue Accounting Research Bulletin No. 33 which reaffirmed the Institute's position on the historical cost basis for the depreciation charge, a position backed by the SEC and the New York Stock Exchange.

Because of continuing dissatisfaction with the means of accounting for inflation The Study Group on Business Income, jointly financed by the Rockefeller Foundation and the Institute, was created in 1947 and was charged to make a "comparative and historical study of income, its concepts and terminology as used in accounting and other fields." [24] The Group, composed of accountants, lawyers, economists, and businessmen, reported in 1952 that financial statements could be meaningful only if expressed in terms of equal purchasing power. The recommendation was opposed by the SEC, FTC, and the Federal Power Commission. The AICPA addressed the issue indirectly in 1953 in connection with issuing Bulletin No. 43, a restatement and revision of all prior bulletins on accounting and "only a bare two-thirds majority was mustered to reprint and thus affirm Bulletin 33. The problem of accounting for inflation kept cropping up in subsequent discussions but was finally dropped from the AICPA Committee agenda in 1958." [25]

Nevertheless, interest in price level adjustments continued. At a seminar at New York University (Hayden Stone Accounting Seminar, December 13, 1962), Thomas G. Higgins, a member of the

Accounting Principles Board and Senior Partner of Arthur Young and Company, expressed the need for adjusting financial statements for price level accounting. He viewed the task as one which would actually substitute price level adjusted reports for historical cost-based reports. He suggested a first phase of five to seven years during which such reports would be optional, but the profession would press for adoption and try to persuade the Congress to modify the tax laws to allow for deductions of depreciation expense based on price adjusted values for depreciable assets. After this trial period

> price-level statements will become official financial statements of all major companies, replacing the conventional, historical dollar statements. But because I think that financial statements based on historical cost may be needed for reference, I would not eliminate them completely. Instead, I would present them as supplementary information at least in the early years of Stage Two [meaning after the trial period].[26]

This revolutionary departure from historically based financial reports coming from a respected member of the profession received little publicity; it was almost 15 years ahead of its time.

In 1963, the AICPA issued a research study on "Reporting the Financial Effects of Price Level Changes" (ARS No. 3). This study, prepared by the research staff of the Institute, provided empirical evidence showing the impact of adjustments for price level change to some 18 corporations of various size and industry characteristics and recommended that the impact of changes in price levels on financial statements be provided as supplementary information to published reports. A public hearing was held attended by representatives of the Financial Executives Institute, National Assocation of Accountants, Security Analysts, American Bankers Association, and other interested parties. After extensive discussion, this group was polled on the adoption of the recommendations of the study; the response was almost entirely negative. The APB decided nevertheless to endorse the recommendations contained in the research study in the form of a "Statement" and not an opinion, the former representing a desirable reporting suggestion wherein it was hoped that over time, it would be adopted and ultimately become required. This was a pious hope. The record shows that practically no American corporation elected to supplement published annual reports with price adjusted financial reports.

The problem refused to disappear and the FASB put the issue on its agenda and in February 1974, issued a Discussion Memorandum. After public hearings, it produced an exposure draft in December 1974. The draft provided for:

a. Continuation of financial reports on an historical basis.
b. Supplementary financial statements reflecting corrections in historical costs into dollars of common purchasing power.
c. The price index to be used is the GNP deflator as a measure of changes in general purchasing power.

In effect the FASB's draft was almost entirely based on the prior work of the APB as contained in its Statement No. 3.

What seems to be the official reaction of the SEC to the FASB's draft appears in "A Notice of proposed amendment to Regulation S-X to require disclosure of certain replacement cost data in notes to financial statements" (S7-579) published on August 21, 1975. The proposed amendment would require registrants to disclose the following in footnotes to financial statements:

Assets—for the fiscal year for which a balance sheet is presented:

a. The estimated current replacement cost inventory at each fiscal year end

b. The estimated current cost of replacing the productive capacity together with the current net replacement cost represented by the depreciable, depletable, and amortizable assets on hand at the end of each fiscal year

Costs and Expenses—for each of two most recent fiscal years:

The approximate amount which cost of sales would have been if it had been calculated by estimating the current replacement cost of goods and services sold at the time when the sales were made.

The approximate amount of depreciation, depletion, and amortization which would have been provided if it were estimated on the basis of average current replacement cost of productive capacity.

At least initially, the presentation of these footnoted data would be labelled "unaudited."

Without directly indentifying the current FASB exposure draft, the SEC proposal stated that:

> . . . the general rate of inflation does not reflect the impact of price changes on a particular company. The impact of such price changes may be substantially greater or less than that indicated by an average or general rate of inflation encompassing all price changes in an economy since it is characteristic of an inflationary economy that specific price relationships realign rapidly and unevenly relative to the general rate of inflation.

The introduction to the guidelines for implementing the proposed rules lists the alternatives which could be used in measuring the effects of inflation on a business entity—use of specific rather than general price indexes, and so on. It observed that:

> In proposing limited supplemental disclosure of replacement costs, the Commission is requiring the presentation of data which reflect the impact of specific price changes of the firm. In so doing, the Commission is not reaching the conclusion that data reflecting historical costs on the basis of general purchasing power units would not be useful nor is it suggesting that these data would not be valuable in analyzing specific price changes. *At the present time, however, the Commission is not proposing to require the presentation of data on a general purchasing power basis.* [Italics supplied]

To this point in time the FASB has not acted.

Foreign Experience

Two developments outside of the United States might well affect the direction of the approach to price level adjustments.

Australia. In June 1975, the Australian Accounting Standards Committee issued an exposure draft titled "Current Value Accounting" which adopts a current value approach to the statement of assets in the balance sheet and also deals with the problems associated with the maintenance of the operating capacity of the firm. Profit measurement is based on the principle of matching revenue and expense, both expressed in current values. Finally, the current value basis would replace the historical cost basis as the only financial reporting method. Dual measurement, that is, historical cost statements along with current values statements, is rejected.

United Kingdom. The Sandilands Committee was set up by the British government in January 1974 to study the case for adjusting financial statements to allow for the effect of inflation. The profession in the U.K. issued a provisional standard (SSAP No. 7, May, 1974) which like the *U.S. Statement No. 3* suggests that general price level adjusted statements (based on the index of retail prices) may be used as supplements to financial statements based on historical costs. It is well to note that unlike the American experience with *Statement No. 3,* a significant number of companies in the United Kingdom did present supplementary reports as suggested by SSAP No. 7.

The Sandilands Committee report in September 1975 followed the Australian pattern; that is, it favored relying upon replacement cost as a basis for reporting.

The justification for replacement cost accounting starts with the view that price level adjustment is only a partial solution to the valuation problem. The key difference between the two approaches lies in their respective definitions of capital. The general price level approach defines capital as a command over goods and services while the replacement cost concept focuses on the reproduction of the means of production—a flow of capital in physical terms. Put another way, the difference lies between maintaining the stock of capital (stewardship) or maintaining the purchasing power of the income flow produced by the stock of capital. It is the latter which has greater utility in evaluating managerial performance from the view of the user of financial reports.[27]

Like the Australian proposal, Sandilands recommends that when they are finally adopted, the current cash-based statements should replace historical cost statements.

Some interesting similarities appear between suggestions for change as they evolved in the United States and the United Kingdom. The change in the United States is marked by a number of attempts to gain adoption of general price level adjusted statements as supplementary to conventional financial reports with practically no acceptance by industry. At a point in time when the FASB was about to require such reports, the SEC proposed that current costs rather than general price level should be used as the basis for supplementary statements and questioned the utility of the FASB approach.

The results that were experienced in the United Kingdom are similar and perhaps more dramatic. Even though the profession in the United Kingdom followed the approach taken in the United States. (modified supplementary statements were not mandated), a significant number of British companies adopted the suggested practice. The report of the Sandilands Committee suggests that the profession did not go far enough. It recommends that current value be adopted in the near future and, more importantly, that current value financial statements replace traditional historical based reports.

What is of interest is the coincidence of both the view and the timing of disclosure of the view of governmental agencies in both the United Kingdom and the United States. Government seems to be saying that the slow deliberate approach of dealing with inflation is moving in the wrong direction. Of more significant consequence is the fact that the accountant in both countries is being told in different ways to sever the umbilical cord to historical costs.

In passing, it might be well to take a moment to see how the government of the United States itself has handled the effects of inflation on national income and product accounts. For years, the inventory value adjustment (IVA) has been used to adjust to current values. It is only recently (October 1975) that the Bureau of Economic Analysis has announced that an adjustment will be made in the estimate of depreciation to convert it to a current cost valuation basis.[28] The action, a very slow deliberate process better suited to the track record of the accounting profession, is so different from the approach used by regulatory bodies.

The Dutch Experience

Much of the literature on current value accounting refers to the experience of the Netherlands in the use of the methodology, particularly as practiced by the Dutch company, Phillips. Indeed, the success of the Netherlands experience often is cited in recommendations for adoption of the current value approach. Current value accounting is not imposed by law or by professional regulation in the Netherlands. The few companies that did adopt the practice did so contrary to existing international standards. Nevertheless, the reporting of the Dutch experience is generally as expressed by one American professor:

> The most important [characteristic], and one which appears to have greatly influenced all facets of Dutch accounting, is that the principles of business economics are developed and interpreted by Dutch accountants as practical guides for accounting and auditing. Purportedly, accounting and financial reporting practices are therefore unfettered by accounting conventions and are constrained only by the principles of business economics and by the Dutch auditor's role in seeing that these principles are considered. The Dutch consider that use of replacement [current] values derives from interpretation of the principles of business economics.[29]

One Dutch accountant has suggested that recent research on reporting practices in the Netherlands "throws some light—as well as much cold water" on whether writings on the Dutch experience do assess the real nature of Dutch accounting. He cites three research studies of annual reports of a large number of listed Dutch companies. The conclusion of these studies suggests that "the very few companies that managed to develop a comprehensive system of current value accounting represent the exception that proves the rule."[30] Partial application of current value was encountered, but the largest numbers by far (38 out of 50 companies in one study) are in essence using historical cost as a basis for financial reporting. There was little difference of opinion in industry and in the profession on the fact that current value accounting is conceptually sound but major problems of implementation limited its adoption. The Dutch, in trying to implement the current value concept, have had difficulties in deriving replacement value for fixed assets, tax allocation, accounting for technological change, reporting holding gains, and the effect on financial structure on the application of current value accounting.

It would appear that what has been described as a system of reporting based on principles of business economics and generally used hardly relates to the Dutch situation or the situation in any country. The current state of affairs in what has been viewed as the "model" country is perhaps best summarized by the chairman of a tripartite committee consisting of representatives of Dutch employers, employees, and the profession charged with the responsibility of codifying generally accepted valuation standards in a statement made in 1974:

> One arrives actually at the conclusion that if you ask an accountant or business economist what the profit is, he will answer: How would you like to have it? . . . The conclusion must be that what business economics has offered us till now cannot be made operational for the work of the committee.[31]

Referring to the apparently endless search for a business economic basis in financial reporting, he said that one is still forced to look for a yardstick "somewhere back in one's mind." [32]

In short, current value accounting is an approach to accounting whose time has perhaps come. It is not devoid of very difficult problems of implementation but a concerted effort might well produce useful results. In fact, motivation for dedicating such effort might well come in a form of defensive action. From Canada comes this observation:

> The only way out of the morass of unfair law suits which threaten to bog us down, is through the production of statements which at least attempt to set forth the fairest current values that it is feasible to produce. The accountant in defending himself, will then have the task of demonstrating why he accepted the valuation he did—instead of having to explain why he used

techniques which a skilled prosecutor suggests are in conflict with some esoteric pronouncements of an Australian accounting body or the confused verdict of an Ontario jury.[33]

INTERNATIONAL ACCOUNTING STANDARDS

Setting international accounting standards creates a number of problems, the difficulty of which is suggested by differences among countries in the:

development of the accounting profession
influence of tax laws on financial accounting
provisions of company laws
requirement of regulatory bodies
prevailing accounting practices.[34]

The appearance of a number of international accounting organizations concerned with an exchange of ideas on financial reporting and with actually establishing international financial reporting standards in response to the growth of international business and a higher level of foreign investment is a matter of concern in the evolution of accounting in the United States.

Some of the important International organizations operating at this time are:

1. International Accounting Standards Committee (IASC). This Committee, set up in 1974 by the international Coordination Committee for the Accountancy Profession, consists of representatives of leading professional bodies of Australia, Canada, France, Germany, Japan, Mexico, the Netherlands, the United Kingdom and Ireland, and the United States as founding members with associate members from 13 other countries. The Committee was chartered to develop basic standards to be observed in presenting audited financial statements and promote worldwide acceptance of its standards.

2. Union Européenne des Experts Comptables, Economique et Financiers (UEC). This European body was founded in 1951 and has

been concerned with the formulation of recommendations on accounting and auditing practices.

3. Group d'Etudes des Experts Comptable de la CEE. An organization formed with the objective of consulting members and making representations to the European Economic Community (EEC) Commission on proposed legislation on accounting and auditing matters.

4. Accountants International Study Group (AISG), organized in 1966, consists of representatives of the professional accounting organizations of the United States, Canada, and the United Kingdom. Its objective is to institute comparative studies on accounting thought and practice in participatory countries, to make reports from time to time, which, subject to prior approval by the sponsoring Institutes, would be issued to members of those Institutes. Some 15 studies have been issued.[35]

The International Accounting Standards Committee (IASC) is perhaps the one organization with significant possible future impact on the development of accounting in the United States. Certain topics are selected for study by subcommittees or working parties. The end product is an exposure draft which, if approved by two-thirds majority of the nine founding member countries, is then addressed to professional bodies entitled to participate in the International Accounting Congresses, as well as governments, security markets, regulatory agencies, and others. After review and modification, if they are deemed necessary, a two-thirds vote (seven of nine members) is necessary before a definitive standard is issued which becomes effective from a date to be stated in the standard. Enforcement of standards is to be achieved by persuasion, and the accounting profession in each member country is expected "to use their best endeavors to achieve adherence to these standards." [36]

The experiences of the EEC in harmonizing accounting standards highlights some of the more specific difficulties which are encountered in setting international standards. The EEC countries are faced with a range of accounting principles that are very sophisticated in some countries and very simplistic ones in others. Additionally, some countries have a tradition of very detailed and regimented approaches to accounting principles, whereas others leave as much as possible to the judgment of individuals. It should be noted that "harmonization" is a word frequently used in stating EEC objectives, be they in addressing accounting standards, the value-added tax, or other common problems. Harmonization is achieved by "Directives of the Community" which do not constitute laws of the member countries but direct the countries to the ends to be achieved. How the individual country chooses to achieve the end result is left to each individual government. In effect, it means that each country must amend its laws to achieve the uniform end result outlined in the Directive.

The first draft of the fourth Directive (of a series of five on company law) deals with annual accounts of limited liability companies. It was issued in 1971, the second draft in 1974, and it is still undergoing discussion. It is well to note that the first draft specified rigid rules patterned very much along the lines of German and French practice. Accordingly, it provided that headings and subheadings under which items in the balance sheet and income statement were to be reported were specified; cost was to be the valuation base with replacement permissible provided that increase in value be shown as revaluation surplus which surplus account cannot be reduced; goodwill must be written off over a maximum of five years, among others. The second draft added a section on consolidated statements but did not specifically require that they be used. It also altered the wording of the first draft from the narrow requirement of preparation of statements in conformity with the principles of "regular and proper accounting" (the German approach) to the concept of "true and fair view" (more in keeping with practice in the Netherlands and the United Kingdom). Finally, the draft suggested that deferred taxes must be disclosed in footnotes, but it does not appear that deferred taxation has to be booked. This was a step in the direction of the practice adopted in the United Kingdom, particularly since the first draft ignored deferred taxes in their entirety.

At the moment, work is continuing on modifying the second draft.

Turning back to the IASC, what is its status and how are its activities impacting on American standards?

A standard on disclosure of accounting policies was issued in 1975, followed by drafts on valuation and presentation of inventories, consolidated financial statements, the equity method, depreciation accounting and information to be disclosed in financial statement. It is in connection with the exposure draft on consolidated financial statements that the issue of the relative authority of the IASC has been raised. The situation can be summarized as follows:

The Financial Executive Institute (FEI), an organization of chief financial officers of large corporations, is concerned about potential conflicts between pronouncements of the IASC and the FASB and has taken the position that, except for the SEC, the FASB is the authoritative accounting standard setting body in the United States.[37]

On June 10, 1975, the Chief Accountant of the SEC stated that, if the IASC issues a final statement including consolidated principles and if the FASB does not issue a contrary statement, the SEC will propose it for comment, amendments to its Regulation S-X.

The FASB response to the SEC in setting forth its position, which was fully seconded by the FEI, was reported as follows:

FASB Chairman Marshall Armstrong voiced grave concern about the Burton letter and prevailed upon the SEC not to propose any amendments to Regulation S-X, in calling attention to the SEC's reply to the IASC draft, stated that the effectiveness of the FASB may be seriously undermined and the Board's efforts for the improvement of financial reporting could be dealt a staggering blow. In addition, Chairman Armstrong pointed out that the organizations who sponsor the FASB could consider the SEC response to IASC as a circumvention of the FASB's recognized authority in the private sector with a more than likely loss of moral and financial support for the board.[38]

The AICPA for its part adopted a resolution on July 24, 1975, which states

If there is no significant difference between an international standard and U. S. practice on a subject, compliance with U. S. generally accepted accounting principles will constitute compliance with the international standard. If there is a significant difference between the two, the AICPA will urge the FASB to give early consideration to reconciling the differences.[39]

Where does this leave us? It can be observed that some foreign countries have established procedures for enforcing IASC standards

(Japan and France); others are debating the issue. In the United States, no such action has been taken. Instead we have opted for acceptance if no significant difference exists between IASC and the standards of the United States, which, of course, is not much of anything. But where there are differences, we are in a situation where a new institution has been added to the process of setting standards. It is complicated by the fact that the AICPA and the FEI (only recently added) have representatives on the IASC committee but the American rule-making body, the FASB, does not. Further, the process of rule making adopted by the IASC is reminiscent of the earlier practices of the APB in this country and is at great variance with the FASB's established practice of "due process" in setting standards. In short, there is a new agency in the picture generally representing the professional accountants in the various countries concerned with setting standards with enough clout to get some countries to enforce their standards and enough to have the SEC once again threaten to act on changes suggested by the IASC if the FASB refuses to act.

One could argue that the conflict between rule-making bodies, international and domestic, is not as real as some would suggest and that the FASB and FEI are overacting. Earlier, reference was made to the EEC and their attempt at harmonizing accounting standards among member countries. That the EEC can exercise pressure on its member countries has been demonstrated a number of times because of their concern with a number of important areas of economic activities. Harmonization in the EEC extends beyond mere accounting standards and, hence, pressures can be exercised. (Witness the intense pressure applied on Italy to adopt the value-added tax.) What can the IASC do to force the adoption of its standards where they conflict with standards of the United States? Joseph P. Cummings, the representative of the United States to the IASC Committee, stated:

> As to whether IASC conflicts with the rule-making body in the United States, the FASB, it is important to recognize that international standards do not override local standards such as APB or FASB Statements. At the outset, the IASC recognized that no country could or would yield its sovereignty in setting standards. The intent is to establish standards of comparison and expose differences to the public. Of course, it would be futile to

establish standards if there is no mechanism to ensure that deviations are disclosed. As a founder member of the IASC, the AICPA, along with the other members, has agreed to ensure that its member auditors satisfy themselves that financial statements comply with the international standards. If the statements do not comply, the auditor's report must cover the differences.[40]

It is this required disclosure of differences, if enforced by the government or the constituent professional society of a country, which is the weapon which the IASC has and which is the central issue yet to be resolved in the United States.

PUBLICATION OF EARNINGS FORECASTS

The final problem addressed relates to disclosure of earnings forecasts. Some snows have fallen since the promise was made in 1972 by William J. Casey, then chairman of the SEC, that guidelines for publishing reports would appear "before the snow falls." A research accountant observed that few of us realized that, when Casey referred to snowfall, he was thinking of Miami. A leading business periodical noted that published profit forecasts was an "idea whose time had come—and gone."

The SEC apparently has not listened to these comments. Its release (33-5581), dated April 28, 1975, on which comments were invited, sets forth reporting requirements for companies making public disclosures of sales, earnings, and earnings per share. To be sure, the proposed standards apply only to *voluntary disclosure* and the definition of forecast is very broad, and includes corporate responses to outsiders' forecasts. Contained in the proposed regulations are standards for the reporting of original forecasts and revisions, but of significant importance are the "safe harbor" rules aimed at limiting a company's legal liability where forecasted results are not achieved. There is an implicit linkage in the provisions of the "safe harbor" rules between published forecasts and internal budgets.

The AICPA, although officially opposed to published forecasts, has been busy doing its homework, perhaps in expectation that such a requirement may be forthcoming. Its Management Advisory Committee has prepared a set of guidelines for the development and preparation of financial forecasts while its Accounting Standards Executive Committee has authorized issuance of its statement of position entitled "Presentation and Disclosure of Financial Forecasts."

I believe it is correct to say that objections to required publication presented by the Institute and financial executives centered on the potential legal liability resulting from the publication of forecasts and on the fear of disclosure of information which might affect the competitive advantage of the company.[41]

The SEC has addressed the problem of legal liability in its "safe harbor" suggestion, and the adequacy of this proposal is not explored here, yet it does indicate a degree of concern and opens up a path to a possible solution.

I should like to address the fear of revealing information of a proprietary nature. Recent literature on the behavior pattern of earnings numbers suggest that a notable fraction of the changes in the variability of earnings is explained by the firm's external economic environment. This comes as no surprise to the experienced executive. Indeed, because of the significant impact of the external economic environment of the firm's operations, each forecasting cycle (which is, in general, an integral part of the budgetary process) normally starts with an outline of the general economic conditions which are likely to constitute the environment for the business operations of the next period. Thus the forecast is, in general, a result of an implicit integration of the assumed external conditions. These external conditions can be and are subdivided between those of a macro nature (broad economic factors including GNP, disposable income, and interest rates) and industry variables. Beyond these external variables are the microeconomic elements, which are factors unique to a firm, such as variations in expenditures for research and development, new product introduction, and marketing and manufacturing strategies.

It is suggested that if published forecasts of earnings were accompanied by an explicit statement of assumptions regarding external economic variables (macro and industry) with no disclosure of micro assumptions, the user would be well served in assessing management's performance ex-ante as well as ex-post. The published assumption, when made, could be related to the user's own subjective estimates and, after the fact, variations from forecast could be analyzed to filter out variation between forecasted and actual earnings by causal factors (external vs. internal).[42]

A LOOK TO THE FUTURE

Prediction is a tricky business, even more so for an accountant whose preoccupation is with history. It is further complicated by the fact that accountants are conservative. In fact, some feel they are born that way, springing from the womb with red pencil in hand! Should we expect anything other than a pessimistic view of the future from a conservative accountant? Surely, the experience of the late sixties, with episodes like the pooling follies, the internal battle with accounting for the investment tax credit, and the mounting number of lawsuits would suggest a bleak outlook. The accountant emerged in the public press with a notoriety which he would have preferred to avoid. Perhaps one reference captures the flavor of the image of the accountant during a period which can be viewed as the low water mark for the profession. A cartoon appearing in *The New Yorker* magazine during this period shows three prosperous officers of a corporation in company with their sombre looking independent auditor. One of the officers, with an understanding smile, states: "In examining our books, Mr. Mathews promises to use generally accepted accounting principles *if you know what I mean!*"

An extreme pessimistic projection would suggest the demise of the accounting profession and a transfer of not only the rule-making role to the government but in addition the actual audit of public corporations by government-employed accountants. Earlier in this paper it was noted that the Congress of the United States gave serious consideration to such a proposal in the discussions which preceded the passage of the Securities Act of 1933.

It is difficult to justify this extreme pessimism. The current trend by government at all levels—municipal, state, and Federal—to turn to the professional CPA to audit financial records of government agencies and even the entire financial reporting system of governments to render objective opinions, thus superseding government-employed auditors, would appear to suggest that the public view of the integrity and competence of the private auditor is superior to that of the government-employed auditor. It would appear that the professional accountant's public image is changing for the better.

On a lighter note, one could use *The New Yorker* magazine again as a barometer of public opinion. A cartoon which appeared early in January 1976 depicted a meeting of the board of directors wherein the chairman puts the issue before his board in the following words, "The question before the board, then, is this: Shall we put out a white paper or cop a plea?" The absence of the outside auditor at the meeting of the board would, I suggest, indicate a better public image for the auditor. Or consider the other professions. The popularity of such television programs as Dr. Marcus Welby, Petrocelli, Kojak, and so forth, could imply that the law, medicine, and crime prevention have reached such low levels of public esteem that they need uplifting through a display of fearless, dedicating public servants, as is suggested by the key roles on view in these programs. The absence of a television program entitled Allistair Bluestone, CPA (no steel rimmed glasses and a full head of hair), defender of the public's and stockholder's rights against corporate hijinks, might suggest that the need for compensation for a poor public image is not there.

A moderately pessimistic view has been suggested by G. J. Benston.[43] Framed in the form of what he calls a behavioral hypothesis, he urges that all the professional accountant has to offer and strive to protect is his "individual reputation for integrity and public esteem so that users of certified reports are assured that these reports were not meant to mislead." Hence, the CPAs will move cautiously in making changes, limiting these changes to uniformity in accounting to avoid management manipulation of net income and minor modification to overcome obvious divergences from economic reality.

I would prefer to take a cautious, optimistic approach for the future of financial reporting in general and, more specifically, for the continuance and growth of professional accounting in its traditional domain, the private sector. I shall explain this position by reference to the several topics discussed in this paper: the institutional structure, a conceptual framework for accounting reporting, disclosure, accounting for inflation, international accounting standards, and published earnings forecasts.

The Institutional Framework

The institutional framework as currently constituted, involving a privately financed standards board but prodded and directed by the SEC, will continue. If we learn from history, it is possible that at a future date the FASB may get into difficulties and, like its predecessor, may have to be replaced. I would hazard the guess that a committee will be appointed, and it will recommend a modified organization with a new name and perhaps a different composition, but the change will be primarily one of form. In this connection, we will continue to utilize the institutional structure employed for this purpose by most democratic countries. The essence of the view is perhaps captured by the suggestion that, when the FASB is replaced, a new body called the Accounting Practices Commission or the APC will be the successor. (The initials "APC" are also identified with a frequently used cold remedy which, while it does not cure the common cold, does give temporary relief.)

Role of the SEC

In a more serious vein, I would argue that the logical government agency to take over the responsibility for establishing accounting standards is the SEC, which is in place and has the legal authority to do so. That it has not undertaken this role can hardly be ascribed to the financial cost of doing the job. The FASB's budget, in the order of $3 to $4 million a year, is not that large, and it could be financed by charges made for the filing of reports with the SEC. I would have to argue that the SEC has developed a very unique and, for itself, a most desirable arrangement. (1) It can dictate the direction of areas in which financial standards should be developed and can exercise its veto to the point of getting the kinds of accounting standards it desires. (2) The ultimate enforcement of accounting standards rests with the SEC, and this reinforces its veto power over standards set in the private sector. (3) It was suggested earlier that a significant part of the loosening of standards with regard to the pooling of interests in acquisition could be attributed to the SEC in accepting reports prepared under these poorer standards. Yet the SEC has brought corporations and CPAs to court on a number of occasions due to the admitted "ability to bury millions of dollars of value and create vast questionable earnings under the magic formula of pooling of interest," [44] and accountants and companies have been sued by stockholders directly. But the SEC has not been sued![45] Whatever the fine legal points in the issue, an arrangement which permits the SEC to be the knight in shining armor or a modern "Mr. Clean" is not about to be changed by the agency.

The Conceptual Framework

Let us turn now to the continuing pursuit of a conceptual framework as a basis for setting accounting standards. Several serious efforts were launched in this connection and the FASB has before it the Trueblood report. It is correct to observe that the most vocal group, that is pointing out the need for a theoretic construct for accounting standards, has been the academic accounting group. The need for a broad framework has also been noted in responses to FASB exposure drafts submitted by large CPA firms wherein the need for such a framework is indicated as a guide for responding to proposal for change. The Trueblood report was not conceived as a structure to be adopted in total, and it seems that piecemeal adoption will proceed, while further study will be needed for other areas. Current movement, slow but steady, in the direction of publishing earnings forecasts and the substitution of current values for historical cost values would suggest that this is the direction being taken.

Rule of Disclosure

With regard to the pressure for greater disclosure in financial reports in areas beyond those under present discussion, I would suggest that such pressures may well diminish. If one accepts what appears to be an emerging view of reduced government involvement in the private sector, then perhaps the push for greater disclosure will abate. The history of the SEC, the prime mover in disclosure, does not show a consistent pattern over time but rather reflects the composition of the Commission and its attitudes toward control in the private sector. There have been periods of intense pressure followed by periods of a more relaxed approach. Then, too, we have chewed off an awful lot of new disclosure items that need to be implemented, and this reinforces the conclusion indicated earlier. The three areas mentioned in this paper—published earnings forecasts, current value accounting, and international accounting standards, to which can be added the reporting problems associated with quarterly financials, lines of business, among others—will be enough to keep both the SEC and FASB fully occupied for the foreseeable future.

CONCLUSION

In short, I would expect that for the rest of this century the profession will continue to grow and expand its activities, both intensively in greater involvement in corporate audits and extensively in active participation in the audit of governmental agencies and organizations. The structure will not change much and disclosure efforts will focus on implementing the proposals for current cost accounting and the publication of earnings forecasts with significant progress in harmonizing international accounting standards. The professional investor will have available more, and, I think, better, information. Whether this will make for better investment decisions, I am not sure. Will it prevent some scoundrel from milking a large number of the stockholders? I am sure it won't!

NOTES

1. L. Goldberg, "The Development of Accounting," *The Australian Accounting Student* (March 1949).
2. Stephen A. Zeff, *Forging Accounting Principles in Five Countries* (Champaign, Ill.: Stripes Publishing Co., 1972), pp. 112-113.

3. Ibid., p. 126.

4. Paper by SEC Commissioner A. A. Sommer, Jr., at the University of Washington, January 21, 1974, p. 2.

5. M. F. Cohen, "The Influence of the SEC Regulation on Accounting Practice," *Accounting Practices of the Seventies* (Boston: Hanover Lamont Corp., 1970), pp. 249-250.

6. *Fifth Annual Report of the Securities and Exchange Commission* (Washington, D.C.: June 30, 1939), p. 121.

7. R. J. Chambers, "The Anguish of Accountants," a paper before the Australian Association of University Teachers of Accounting, New Zealand, August 1971.

8. J. C. Burton, "The SEC and the Accounting Profession: Responsibility, Authority and Progress," *Institutional Issues in Public Accounting*, R. R. Sterling, ed. (Lawrence, Kansas: Scholars Book Co., 1974), p. 275.

9. C. A. Lamden, "Comments" on Burton's paper, ibid., p. 276.

10. C. T. Horngren, "Accounting Principles, Private or Public Sector?" *Journal of Accountancy* (May 1972), p. 39.

11. R. T. Baker, "Why Aren't We Solving Our Problems in Accounting Principles?" *Financial Executive* (January 1972), p. 16.

12. A. A. Sommer, Jr., paper delivered at the University of Washington, January 21, 1974, pp. 6-7.

13. J. C. Burton "The SEC and the Changing World of Business," *Journal of Contemporary Business* (Spring 1973), p. 55.

14. H. E. Kapnick, "Changes Needed tc Meet the Challenges of the Future," *Corporate Financial Reporting: The Issues, The Objectives and Some New Proposals,* Rappaport and Revsine, EDS., (N.Y.: Commerce Clearing House, 1972), p. 24.

15. Cited in R. P. Brief, "The Accountant's Responsibility in Historical Perspective," a paper presented at the American Accounting Association, New Orleans, La., August 20, 1974, p. 21.

16. J. Shank, "The Pursuit of Accounting Standards, Whither and Whence," *Journal of Contemporary Business* (Spring 1973), p. 87.

17. *The Wheat Report, Establishing Accounting Standards, Report of the Study Committee on the Establishment of Accounting Principles* (New York: American Institute of Certified Public Accountants, March 1972), p. 18.

18. *The New York Times* (June 25, 1972), cited by Brief, op. cit., p. 5.

19. Zeff, op. cit., pp. 115-116.

20. G. J. Benston, "Required Disclosure and the Stock Market: An Evaluation of the Securities Exchange Act of 1934," *American Economic Review* (March 1973), p. 153.

21. J. W. Buckley, "Public Accounting: The Dynamics of Occupational

Change, A Response," "Institutional Issues in Public Accounting," op. cit., pp. 27-29.

22. G. Chandra, "Information Needs of Security Analysts," *Journal of Accountancy* (December 1975), pp. 66-68.

23. W. H. Beaver, "What Should be the FASB's Objectives?" *Journal of Accountancy* (August 1973), p. 53. See also L. Hagerman, T. F. Keller, and R. J. Petersen, "Accounting Research and Accounting Principles," *Journal of Accountancy* (March 1973), pp. 54-55.

24. Zeff, op. cit.

25. Idem.

26. T. G. Higgins, "Price Level Depreciation," *Hayden Stone Accounting Forum* (New York: New York University, December 13, 1962).

27. R. A. Hill, "Constant Purchasing Power of Replacement Costs," *The Accountant* (November 27, 1975), p. 607.

28. Allan H. Young, "New Estimates of Capital Consumption Allowances, Revision of GNP in the Benchmark," *Survey of Current Business* (October 1975), p. 14.

29. G. M. Scott, "A Business Economic Foundation for Accounting: The Dutch Experience," *Accounting and Business Research,* Autumn 1971, London, quoted by J. W. Muis, "Current Value Accounting in the Netherlands: Fact or Fiction," *The Accountant's Magazine* (November 1974), p. 377.

30. Ibid.

31. Ibid., p. 378.

32. Ibid., p. 379.

33. H. Ross, "The Nature of Professional Responsibility," in "Institutional Issues in Public Accounting," op. cit., p. 238.

34. *Accounting Standards for Business Enterprise Throughout the World* (Chicago, Ill.: Arthur Andersen & Co., 1974), p. 3.

35. C. J. Jones, "Accounting Standards—A Blind Alley?" *Accounting and Business Research* (Autumn 1975), pp. 274-275.

36. *The Accountant's Magazine* (March 1974), pp. 75-77.

37. *Bulletin,* Financial Executives Institute (September 12, 1975), p. 1.

38. Idem.

39. Idem.

40. Joseph P. Cummings, "Forging International Accounting Standards," a paper presented at the International Accounting Seminar, University of Illinois, June 1975, p. 9.

41. A. T. Kearney, *Public Disclosure of Business Forecasts* (New York: Financial Executives Research Foundation, 1973).

42. Amir Barnea, Simcha Sadan, and Michael Schiff, "Conditional Perfor-

mance Review," *Management Accounting* (November 1975), and by the
same authors, "Afraid of Publishing Forecasts?" forthcoming issue of
The Financial Executive.

43. G. J. Benston, "Accountant's Integrity and Financial Reporting,"
Financial Executive (August 1975), pp. 10-14.

44. Kapnick, op. cit., p. 24.

45, In passing, it should be noted that the SEC was sued by an accounting
firm, Arthur Andersen & Co., in connection with ASR No. 148, August
24, 1973, dealing with treasury stock acquisition in the two-year period
prior to an acquisition. The SEC backed off.

SEVEN

The Evolving Role of Business Information

John Diebold

Chairman, The Diebold Group, Inc.

Since the beginning of modern society, the exchange of timely and accurate information has been critical in conducting business and public affairs. The eleventh-century Doomsday Book, a censuslike compendium, was one of the key elements in William the Conqueror's efforts to bring order to his newly won Britain. Lord Rothschild's early knowledge regarding the British victory at Waterloo in 1815 enabled him to buy securities at favorable prices on the London Exchange, a contributing factor to the growth of the great banking house of Rothschild. Similarly, the first United States census, taken in 1810, was a milestone in the development of a systematic data base for business and government here. However, highly precise business information, as a concept, and as the basis for a technology and a set of practices, is relatively NEW, as are the formalization of "management control" techniques as we know them today, even though flourishing economies with fairly large companies, such as the vast Mediterranean trade network, at its peak from 1550 to 1600, were operating with little application of such tools.

Each step in the development of a technology for more speedy and systematic handling of information was indeed a milestone. The typewriter, the telephone, the transatlantic cable, the dictating machine were all milestones in enabling business to deal more effectively with information. These and other developments recapitulated on Exhibit I each created its own "revolution" in accounting, in communication, in make-up of the work force.

These developments *coincided with* and *facilitated* the growth of large-scale American businesses and were no doubt important in supporting the introduction of systematic management procedure, much of which is surprisingly recent. (It was not until the early 1920s that Alfred P. Sloan began applying the new concepts of centralized control and decentralized management to the troubled General Motors Corporation.) But the fundamental developments of management during this period were not concerned with information; they were related to concepts of organization, of industrial engineering, and, in later stages, to concepts of human and labor relations. It is since the invention and subsequent widespread utilization of the electronic digital computer by business and public institutions that business information—its organization, handling and use—has become a pivotal factor in the success or failure of a business, or of an industry.

It is a subtle, qualitative difference to which I refer, but one whose reality is attested to by the increasing role for business information and its technology, its impact, and its universality that we shall be considering in this paper.

In this discussion, I will deal with the following concepts and areas: First, the significant developments and achievements in processing information that, between 1950 and 1976, changed the role of this business information from an adjunct to a central factor in business organization and management. But in spite of these advances we so far have seen only the tip of the iceberg in terms of the impact of information technology on business and society. Second, technology applications that can be viewed as "Straws in the Wind," pointing toward some of the broader impacts and achievements anticipated in the next several decades. Third, the increasingly difficult and questionable value of separating the two concepts, "business" information and "social" information. Fourth, some of the opportunities, problems, and questions that these developments must create for businessmen, public officials, and individuals.

EXHIBIT I

Early Milestones in Handling of Business Information

1833   Prototype of modern typewriter invented in France by Xavier Progin.

1876   First practical telephone invented by Alexander Grahan. Bell.

1879   First dial telephone with automatic switching system. Thomas A. Edison recorded the human voice.

1881   Bell demonstrated use of the first practical recording machine.

1888   Dictating machines came into general commercial use.

1890   Herman Hollerith devised a series of electrical machines, which when fed data on punched cards, performed adding and counting operations, and reduced the time required to take the national census from seven to three years.

1915   First nationwide telephone hookup was made from New York to Chicago, and New York to San Francisco. First transatlantic radio call, New York to Paris.

1919   Electric synchronized time clock introduced.

1920   Printing Tabulator introduced.

1928   Punched card was made to hold 80 columns, nearly doubling previous capacity.

1931   Alphabetic accounting machines and accounting machines that multiply and divide introduced.

1935   First commercially successful electric typewriter marketed by IBM.

1942   First transatlantic call was made via cable.

1948   IBM's first large-scale digital calculating machine was made available.

DEVELOPMENTS TO 1976

The development of a technology for business information and a "science" for its application has been one of the greatest success stories of our time, both in terms of pure technological accomplishment and in terms of impact on the way business and society is managed and operates.

The field, however defined, has chalked up a phenomenal record of technical accomplishment in the past 20 years. Some examples and trend lines relating to performance and cost may help bring home the truly remarkable record:

- Over the last decade the speed of handling a transaction has increased by a factor of 10 every four years.
- In the mere half second that it takes for spilled coffee to drip from table to floor, today's large computer can:
  —Debit 2000 checks to 300 different bank accounts, *and*
  —Examine electrocardiograms of 100 patients, *and*
  —Score 150,000 answers on 3000 exams concurrently evaluating the effectiveness of the questions, *and*
  —Figure the payroll for a company with 1000 employees.
- Between 1960 and 1970, the cost of an electronic function, such as a transistor, declined 99.9 percent—just as if the price of a $50,000 house were to fall to $50.

Chart 1 dramatizes the accomplishments that have already been achieved (and also the future performance capabilities for which the technology is largely in existence). The chart shows the results of higher speed, lower cost, greater reliability, and, therefore, better usability of the technical base for even more sophisticated and universally applied information systems.

Now that we have made these achievements, there are some who feel the technology is slowing down, maturing. While I agree that we have a long way to go in applying simply the technology we already have, I do not think that we are undergoing a technological

Chart 1. Trends and projections of cost effectiveness of computers and communications

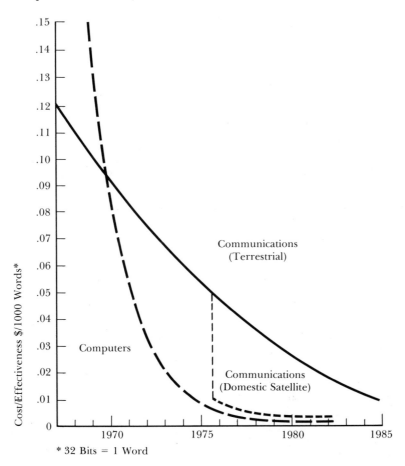

* 32 Bits = 1 Word

maturing. Rather, I share the view espoused by John Pierce of Bell Labs:

> After 25 years of unparalleled technical progress, the computer industry is ready to enter its infancy.

In part, this potential for further progress in a field that has already exceeded all expectations can be explained by the nature of technological development. Lewis Branscomb has pointed out that:

> The apparent exponential development of a technology, over time, is really a succession of different technologies contributing to the same end: as each individual technology (e.g., vacuum tubes, transistors, etc.) reaches its limit, a new applicable technology (e.g., large-scale integration) picks up where the other left off. The apparently exponential rate of progress in a technology, evaluated over decades of time, in fact represents a succession of different technologies devoted to the same useful purpose.

The most recent of these technologies that has been developed for the field of information systems is the microprocessor. But other technologies are being developed that promise we will make ever greater achievements in the next 20 years, even in "basic hardware." These include an electronic-beam-addressed memory. The storage target is a silicon wafer with an array of silicon dioxide islands on one surface on which an electron beam can write, read, and erase. The result is a further major increase in the speed of data processing, and reduction of cost. Magnetic bubbles are being developed that can be used for memory, switching, and logic. They are low-cost, low-power devices. They are versatile and potentially capable of reaping the full advantage of integrated circuits.

Perhaps equally pertinent as new developments of this kind are the major advances that can be gained from the better use of existing technology, in three important areas. The use of *software,* broadly defined as the ability to use, comprehend and communicate with information technology products, can be improved. This area has the greatest need for development and the greatest potential, as it continues to be basically a "handicraft industry," for the programming of computers is still a painstaking job that requires large amounts of time and effort. Developments here will bring about a much more "natural" flow of information in the organization. With some exceptions, the computer today remains a resource that most people in business (at every level) find hard to understand and deal with, and for which some special training is required. Contrast this with the telephone, which has become a system used with ease by everyone. The aim of software development in the coming years will be to make an information system as easy to deal with as the telephone. Thus, instead of having to "organize around the computer" it should be possible for the hardware to be applied to suit the needs of the user for information. There should be *further progress made to develop new, small devices* to deal with data input and output. Like software, the latter provide a means of bridging the gap between the computer-communication system and the everyday user. The airline ticket agent and the savings bank teller "converse" directly with their information system when a transaction takes place. The next years will see a proliferation of inexpensive devices that will allow many information users direct access to the total information system that services them. Also, we should apply our present knowledge to incorporate existing information technology into "everyday" products, from cameras to kitchen appliances, as is done at present to produce sewing machines.

Another way to appreciate the accomplishments of the information technology field is its growth as a business and a national resource. Information technology has been a major contributor to our economic growth and has become perhaps America's third or fourth largest manufacturing and service industry, so diverse and complex that it can be measured in a multiplicity of ways. (Our superiority in this technology, recognized worldwide, has prompted other countries to engage in a host of attempts, often ill-conceived and expensive, to develop national or regional computer industries.)

Information technology comprising computers and communications probably is *the* industry in which the United States has the greatest technological and applications lead over the rest of the world. In spite of our relatively severe export curbs, in 1975 the net export surplus for the industry has been estimated at $2.3 billion. At the same time, the *application* of information technology has had a pervasive "how could we have survived without" impact in a number of ways. In management, in both the public and private sectors, information technology is the *sine qua non* for coping with the data endemic to an increasingly complicated world. In countless operations, current technology lowers the cost of, and provides the sheer physical means to deal with, the workload—from handling several billion bank checks a year, to directing and accounting for countless telephone calls, to tracking and controlling NASA space flights. This same technology delivers to scientists, researchers, and engineers a tool that both tremendously increases their potential productivity and the interest and challenge of their work.

Notwithstanding this unique record, it is only now that information technology is entering the take-off phase. In spite of the importance and prevalence of computers, the controversy inherent in the question of availability and the interpretation of data have relegated most current uses of computer communications and related technology and know-how to *the periphery* of the concerns of management. Computers are applied to determine *how* a process is achieved, rather than to help us assess *what* is done; for instance, they process checks but do not eliminate the need for the entire billing involving the cycle from check writing to check processing. Information technology now is applied to processes which *directly* affect only a small proportion of the population.

During the next quarter-century we will see:

A shifting emphasis to *what* is done rather than how the process is accomplished.

Applications that directly affect a large part of the population.

Consumer as well as capital goods that are based on information technology.

Major *public policy* questions arising, as business information and social information grow increasingly intertwined.

INFORMATION TECHNOLOGY'S BROADENING INPUT

These developments in the field of information will be accompanied by, and to some extent, brought about by a merging of information areas that were formerly largely separate and distinct.

This trend will gradually make the use of the term "business information" as applied to information systems obsolete. By 2001 "business information systems" as such will be inseparable from larger flows involving total use of information technology. Evolving business systems will increasingly integrate all relevant sectors of the community and economy into a series of defined systems related more to subject matter than to sector identity. To illustrate, in the past information systems tended to be identified by titles such as Business-Government, Business-Consumer, Business-Business, and Business-Employee. These have been used as standards for division emphasizing sector identity. However, already such a closed system often is not capable of application to existing and projected highly diverse, yet unified, multi-component information systems. Two examples already in initial phases of functioning are:

A banking system integrating customers of all kinds—business employers, government payees, government regulators, suppliers—into one total money management system.

Retail distribution handled through automated facilities that tie consumer, retailer, and manufacturer together and link the latter to one banking system at appropriate points for payments.

One such "system" may thus contain merchants' catalog and inventory information, profiles on individual customer desires and characteristics (perhaps including such minutiae as shoe size or home characteristics of a given customer), customer asset and credit information, census type data on customer family and neighborhood characteristics. It will be logical to link such a "system" with others that relate to a person's employment, health and medical history, tax and financial information, and so forth. By the same token, these "systems" will overlap with others that have similar breadth on the institutional and organizational side. Such a system would be used to effect transactions between banks, businesses, and governments, and storing data related to these transactions. There will be obvious points of overlap between these multi-component systems, such as where an insurance company makes payments to a hospital on behalf of a business whose employee is receiving treatment.

Information technology and basic logic will thus meld an increasingly large number of separate sectors of daily living into integrated information systems that overlap with each other and which have elements of individual, government, business and institutional information. As this occurs, new ways of serving consumer and business needs will create new industries, the development of which will provide opportunities. At the same time, these developments based on information technology will obsolete or significantly change the way in which some existing industries and institutions function.

Such developments occur over fairly long periods of time. As a result, one can see early manifestations, or straws in the wind, of what can be expected in the future. For example, some industries whose characteristics have been fundamentally changed already by information technology:

Securities Trading

In my first book 24 years ago, I postulated an electronic system that directly connected buyers and sellers of securities and retained the necessary trading information to allow these traders to deal among themselves, without the frantic mayhem of a busy day on the floor of a stock exchange. In the over the counter market, such a system exists. Under pressure from the SEC and from progressive brokerage firms, even the stock exchanges are facing reality and allowing technology to shake an obsolete system. The few major brokerage firms with technical sophistication have captured the volume business in the securities field, and have permanently altered the structure of Wall Street securities trading.

Communication

On the one hand, the twin developments of the low price telephone communications system and the ability to send data to, from, and between computers has largely made the telegraph in its traditional form obsolete. Western Union survives not because of its telegraph monopoly, but only to the extent it has been able to piggy back onto some of the new technology based information and communication services. On the other hand, a whole new industry—data communications—has come into being, which has provided opportunities not only for ATT but, for the first time in recent history, for other, new companies in what was formerly a captive field.

Printing

Product line and printing equipment have totally changed over the past 20 years, a good example of multiple impact of information technology on *all* aspects of an industry:

"Hot lead" printing is being replaced by computer type setting and graphics. The increasing introduction of visual display terminals—really the visible manifestations of what is in computer storage—are completely changing the jobs performed in the newsroom by reporters, editors and clerical employees, as well as the work of those in the press room, photoengravers, stereotypers and typographers.

Additionally, geographic limits on printing plant locations will be greatly reduced by transmission of "ready to print" plates. For many years the *Wall Street Journal* has been printed in multiple locations across the country. Currently New York City's two largest papers—*The Times* and the *Daily News*—are developing production facilities outside of the city.

Such new technology also changes the products that the consumer receives. Local and suburban newspapers become economical, as do "regional" editions of what were formerly nationwide publications that ran the same stories and advertisements in Florida as in Alaska.

Additionally, in the printing industry, general interest magazines, which in the past were seen by up to 40 million people an issue, already have, or may soon be wiped out by the continual growth of all electronic media.

Banking

The changes wrought by information technology in the banking field already affect all areas:

public policy
consumer service
structure of the banking industry

Introduction of a data terminal directly linked to the central information system of a bank has made virtually any location a potential branch bank—a supermarket, a store front, even a telephone booth. Large banks are thus in a position to expand quickly and inexpensively into any geographic area. The same system also enables these banks with sophisticated information technology capabilities to provide better and faster basic services than many small, local establishments.

The result is a shake-up in the structure of the banking industry and logical developments that increasingly challenge the whole structure of regionally separate banking institutions that forms the public policy behind our current banking laws.

When we consider the future it is just as valuable to think about what has *not* happened that might have or could have happened.

Education: the promise and potential for electronic teaching aids, expected by many in the 1960s, has not yet materialized. Teaching methods and materials remain much the same, influenced more by xerography than the ability of communications to bring the computer into every classroom.

Information utilities providing inexpensive central computing power and access to large banks of professional, technical, or business information have had only a faltering start in spite of the great expectations in the 1960s.

For these and others, the technology is there, at affordable cost. What has been lacking is the right combination of entrepreneurial know-how and drive

properly conceived product and service combinations

necessary, widespread marketing effort to show consumers the savings in cost and time, and to overcome the resistance of institutions and professions organized around the existing frameworks.

Straws in the Wind

For further "Straws in the Wind" of how information technology has an increasingly *direct* effect on the individual, we might look at some of the numerous "encounters" with computers that a person might have in the course of his or her day.

Breakfast

Watching television, one sees a computer based weather forecast.

Driving to work

Siemens, a German firm is experimenting with inquiry system for automobile drivers. By consulting a dashboard-mounted unit, the driver will be able to select the best route, taking into consideration traffic, weather and road conditions.

Commuting

By bus, meters controlled by small computers count incoming passengers, log in money, count outgoing passengers and make change. At the end of a day, they give complete financial accounting.

By train, in San Francisco's new rapid transit system, everything from ticketing, to scheduling, to actual operation of the equipment is computerized.

Traffic

Microprocessors control traffic lights in small intersections. Working from information gathered in the street, they vary algorithms to change the lights according to the time of day and traffic conditions.

Ordering Consumer Goods

Simpsons-Sears in Toronto has been using a computer system with which mail ordering for known-value merchandise like Arrow shirts can be done by touch tone dialing. Simpsons-Sears customers can order virtually all of the 80,000 items in the catalogue by talking directly to the computer, whose voice response verifies the order.

Obtaining Medical Care

Scientists have created a computer program that can prescribe treatment for various ailments. From questionnaires the scientists learned that the computer had nearly 100 percent accuracy in prescribing treatments recommended by specialists.

Planning a New Home or Office Building

Architects can use computers programmed to generate pictures or drawings to show a prospective building in various settings, enabling an observer to "walk" through the scene. Computers can also produce detailed building plans.

Receiving Mail

Computers are used in campaigns to write "personal letters" to voters. The letters are designed to fit issues into particular precincts or to appeal to special interest groups. A computer written letter from a candidate to Green Bay, Wisconsin voters might talk about the high cost of living in terms of "The dollar you take to Prange's Department Store," a local firm.

Straws in the wind for information technology as a key component in consumer as well as capital goods are already with us:

Wrist watch calculators provide a handy, wearable, discrete way for shoppers to add up grocery bills, businessmen to figure bank balances.

Polaroid SX-70 is a pocket-sized folding single lens reflex camera which uses 400 transistors to permit one-step photography. The transistors control everything from flashbulb selection to exposure control and allow a color print to be produced in one and a half seconds,

The Ford Motor Company plans to introduce computers into its automobiles in 1979. Microcomputer-run controls will cut fuel consumption by as much as 20 percent,

Singer sewing machines are now using microprocessor elements to control and select stitch patterns and sizes, allowing the user many more alternatives and greater ease in sewing,

Electronic games as Christmas presents stimulate and educate both children and adults. The computer assembly kit gives kids an opportunity to make a computer that can predict the weather, make translations, and teach programming.

The public policy implications of information systems' and technology's extension into ever-increasing areas of business and individual life already have made themselves felt, but so far only as forerunners of increasingly more difficult future problems.

Privacy

As information technology becomes more cost effective and as the comprehensiveness of systems increases, it will become increasingly hard to balance the conflicting pressures of economy, service, and the individual's need for privacy and recourse to the data about him that the system contains.

Business regulation

The banking industry is only one example where regulations reflecting practices and technology of one era must be modified, without at the same time unwittingly giving up principles and goals that remain valid.

Fostering the computer related industry in the United States

Information technology is one of the fields in which the United States leads the world. Other countries, recognizing the importance of the field, have spent millions subsidizing their national computer related industries and have devised extensive efforts to promote these industries. In contrast, the United States government has no national policy in this regard and has taken many actions that appear basically counter productive.

EVOLVING BUSINESS OPPORTUNITIES AND PROBLEMS

The evolving role of systems and information technology into increasingly broad spheres of activity will continue to be one of the most fruitful sources of opportunity for business and social betterment. The same process will cause significant problems to companies in affected industry areas which do not aggressively adjust to change or which place their bets on the wrong approach.

One of the most fundamental challenges for business is how can companies quickly and adequately adjust to the vulnerability/ opportunity that information technology represents for them.

On the information systems side, even the most sophisticated users of computer and communications systems have been accustomed to dealing with well known vendors providing a full range of services to help the user successfully apply the new technology. Now and in the future, these users will be increasingly faced by new high cost/ performance system components (from central computer to commu- nications channel to input/output terminal) that individually may be attractive but which the user must put together into a system. Dealing with the risks and opportunities of these new developments is a bigger challenge than most users foresee.

The development of multi-company or multi-sector business infor- mation systems will be a major factor in corporate success. As the reach of information systems logically expands beyond the data readily available to a single company, it will be important to have the means for organizing the larger, multicomponent system that is needed. Where progress along these lines has been made—in the commercial banking or the medical information field—it has usually been with the support of some larger entity (the Federal Reserve Bank or the National Institutes of Health) or one or two industry leaders forcing the pace. It is probable that in industries where similar cooperation is needed in the future, some catalytic agent will be needed. This may be either an agent selected by the industry, or perhaps a new competitor who recognizes the opportunity and is prepared to do an "end run." One example of where a major change appears to me to be imminent is in the credit card field. For an individual to carry multiple credit cards today should be an anachronism, and yet there continue to be multiple systems with only some overlap: bank cards, travel and entertainment cards, oil company cards, car rental and airline cards, chain store cards, department store cards, and so forth. Proponents of each system profess their uniqueness and individuality, but consolidation is inevitable.

Beyond information systems, a new challenge for business is to organize to apply in its product design and production processes the amazing new capabilities of information technology components. This will require for some industries a major revamping of their product development and engineering organizations to introduce the skills relating to these devices and, more important perhaps, to achieve receptivity within the organization for what results.

Broadening of information systems and changes in the resulting product or service will cause changes in the relationship of a business with its customers. The successful company will have to recognize how its pricing, advertising, packaging, marketing, and overall image will have to be adjusted. For example, how should food company packaging be modified if computer coded pricing that the consumer cannot read is accepted at the supermarket level. Or how should medical services be priced if central, communications based diagnostic services become widespread.

A final, often overlooked business problem is the need to anticipate information technology developments in related fields that will have severe competitive impacts on other products or services. Xerographic reproduction created a whole new industry, but it caused convulsions in the carbon paper and parts of the printing equipment fields. Credit cards and proliferation of checking accounts have impacted the money order business. Communications developments have revolutionized the magazine publishing field, not only through television but through the more indirect effect on mail rates. Business in all fields will increasingly need a "technology look out system" or an early warning apparatus that not only identifies new developments but also properly evaluates their impact.

Some of these tendencies are summarized in Exhibit II which shows six basic ways in which the evolving role of information technology will affect business and gives some examples of how such changes will affect various industries.

Exhibit II

NATURE OF SECOND PHASE INFORMATION TECHNOLOGY IMPACT

Industry/Business Field	Nature of Change Basic Product/Service	Consumer User Interface	Production Process	Product Content/Components	Product Has Information Technology Capability Base	Impacted By Changes In Other Industries
Consumer Durables			x	x		
Broadcasting and Periodicals Publishing	x	x	x			
Advertising					x	x
Banking—Credit	x	x	x		x	
Communications:						
Telephone	x	x		x	x	x
Mail		x	x			x
Retailing		x				x
Capital Goods and Production Equipment			x	x		x
Transportation			x			x
Education	x	x	x		x	
Medical Equipment	x	x	x	x	x	

EVOLVING PUBLIC POLICY QUESTIONS

Public policy implications of a field as fast moving and encompassing as this are legion. I would simply like to cite five that appear to be of particular current importance.

1. How do we maintain a climate to allow the next steps in information technology development and application to be as dynamic as that of the last 20 years? We must recognize that success involved high risks and we must assure that we retain the necessary incentives for industry and individuals to take such risks. And also assure that we do not create a new system of disincentives to punish success or make it unworthwhile.

2. How do we need to modify our laws and regulations to recognize new opportunities and yet maintain the basic principles that remain applicable?

Antitrust must recognize the need for intercompany and interindustry cooperative efforts.

Privacy must be protected.

Communications regulation must recognize the ever changing role of all types of communication.

Industry regulators (such as banking and transportation) must take a broad view of their fields in light of impending information technology developments.

To help come to grips with some of these problems, we at The Diebold Institute for Public Policy Studies are organizing a new seminar series on the public policy questions raised by a "universal" information technology environment. The series will deal with two interrelated areas:

How to maintain the dynamic and entrepreneurial environment to continue the growth and benefits of the information technology field?

How to protect against the problems and dangers it may carry with it?

3. Concerning the cost incidence of future information sys-

tems, such as mail and phone, how should the cost of "common systems" be divided among the various user categories? This is already a problem, but it will increase as unified systems are extended.

4. How should we retain judgment and perspective in a computer propelled world? For example, after the oil embargo and price increases, nearly all computer forecasts of the impact predicted results that for many nations were "unacceptable." Belief in such forecasts, combined with an aggressive spirit, could have led any number of countries to military actions. In reality, the actual results have been very different. Mechanistic systems cannot easily introduce sufficient variables and counterinfluences into forecasts when dealing with new and unprecedented developments.

5. How do we deal with the "catastrophe of aggravated risk" as more and more systems are monolithic and increasingly all our "chips" are on them (for example, the 1965 power failure in the northeastern United States)? To quote Lewis Branscomb of IBM ". . . by improving the quality of a system and diminishing the risk of *local failure* in that system, we seem to automatically encounter a small but important risk of *catastrophic failure.*"

There is no simple way to deal with the opportunities and problems inherent in the evolving role of information technology. The first and ever-present need is to recognize the breadth, which I am sure I have understated in this commentary. But with such a vast scope, the basic need is for generalization of knowledge on all aspects of information technology. This includes use and interaction of products, knowledge of capability and limitations of systems, feeling of confidence in dealing with information related systems, and security to question without awe when conclusions should be questioned.

To achieve this technology's potential with fewest drawbacks, each person, ideally, should become as familiar and comfortable with the products and services created by the technology as he or she is with a telephone, television set, or typewriter. For this, we must have education at all levels, beginning at as early an age as possible and functioning on a continuing basis.

The first step to achieve this is to recognize that the evolving role of business information involves breaking the conceptual boundaries that separate business information from "nonbusiness" information. The real and inevitable evolution of business information is as an integrated element in a community system.

OTHER BOOKS IN THIS SERIES:

BUSINESS PROBLEMS OF THE SEVENTIES
Edited by Jules Backman, Research Professor of Economics, New York University

This volume contains contributions by the following outstanding authorities in the field:
A Foreword by Harold S. Geneen. Chairman and Chief Executive Officer, International Telephone and Telegraph Company
Martin R. Gainsbrugh, Formerly Chief Economist, The Conference Board
Solomon Fabricant, Professor of Economics, New York University
C. Fred Bergsten, Senior Fellow. The Brookings Institution
Simon H. Whitney, Visiting Professor of Economics, Baruch College, City University
M. A. Adelman, Professor of Economics, Massachusetts Institute of Technology
Jesse W. Markham, Harvard University, Charles Edward Wilson Professor of Business Administration
Lee Loevinger, Partner, Hogan and Hartson, Attorneys at Law

ADVERTISING AND SOCIETY
Edited by Yale Brozen, Professor of Business Economics, Graduate School of Business, University of Chicago

This volume contains contributions by the following other scholars in the field:
Daniel J. Boorstin, Smithsonian Institution
Lester G. Telser, University of Chicago
Phillip Nelson, State University of New York at Binghamton
Harold Demsetz, University of California at Los Angeles
Richard A. Posner, University of Chicago
Robert Pitofsky, New York University, Georgetown Law School

John A.P. Treasure, J. Walter Thompson Company
Philip Kotler, Northwestern University

MULTINATIONAL CORPORATIONS, TRADE AND THE DOLLAR
Edited by Jules Backman and Ernest Bloch, New York University

This volume contains contributions from the following other scholars in the field:
Charles P. Kindleberger, Ford Professor of Economics, Massachusetts Institute of Technology
Raymond Vernon, Herbert F. Johnson Professor of International Business Management, Graduate School of Business Administration, Harvard University
Arnold W. Sametz, Professor of Finance, New York University

LABOR, TECHNOLOGY, AND PRODUCTIVITY
Edited by Jules Backman, Research Professor of Economics, New York University

This volume contains contributions by the following other scholars in the field:
Emanuel Stein, Professor of Economics, Humanities, and Social Sciences, New York University
David L. Cole, Chairman, National Commission for Industrial Peace
Peter F. Drucker, Marie Rankin Clarke Professor of Social Science, Claremont Graduate School, Claremont, California
John W. Kendrick, Professor of Economics, The George Washington University

LARGE CORPORATIONS IN A CHANGING SOCIETY
Edited by J. Fred Weston, Professor of Business Economics, Graduate School of Management, University of California, Los Angeles

This volume also contains contributions by the following leading scholars in the field:
Oscar Grusky, Professor of Sociology, UCLA
Marc Nerlove, Professor of Economics, University of Chicago
Oliver E. Williamson, Professor of Economics, University of Pennsylvania
Richard A. Posner, Professor of Law, University of Chicago

Sidney M. Robbins, Professor of Finance, Columbia University

Robert B. Stobaugh, Professor of Business Administration, Harvard University

Neil H. Jacoby, Professor of Economics and Policy, Graduate School of Management, UCLA

Michael Granfield, Assistant Professor of Business Economics, Graduate School of Management, UCLA

Ronald H. Coase, Professor of Economics, University of Chicago Law School

SOCIAL RESPONSIBILITY AND ACCOUNTABILITY
Edited by Jules Backman, Research Professor of Economics, New York University

This volume also contains contributions by the following other scholars in the field:

A Foreword by Harold S. Geneen, Chairman and Chief Executive Officer, International Telephone and Telegraph Corporation

James M. Hester, Rector, the United Nations University, Tokyo, Japan

Juanita M. Kreps, Vice-President, Duke University

James B. Duke, Professor of Economics, Duke University

Oskar Morgenstern, Professor of Economics, New York University

Eleanor Bernert Sheldon, President, Social Science Research Council

Robert Parke, Director, Center for Coordination of Research on Social Indicators, Social Science Research Council

David F. Linowes, Partner, Laventhol Krekstein Horwath & Horwath, Worldwide Auditors and Consultants

Harry Schwartz, Visiting Professor of Medical Economics, Faculty of Medicine, Columbia University

Roger G. Kennedy, Vice-President, Ford Foundation

Ingo Walter, Professor of Economics and Finance, New York University

BUSINESS-GOVERNMENT RELATIONS
Edited by Alan Heslop, Dean of the Faculty, Claremont Men's College.

This volume contains contributions from the following specialists in the field:

A Foreword by Harold S. Geneen, Chairman and Chief Executive Officer, International Telephone and Telegraph Corporation

Herbert Stein, Professor of Economics, University of Virginia

Milton Friedman, Professor of Economics, University of Chicago
Irving Kristol, Professor of Urban Values, New York University
Daniel J. Haughton, Former Chairman of the Board, Lockheed Aircraft
    Corporation
William F. Buckley, Jr., Editor, *The National Review*
Walt W. Rostow, Professor of Economics and History, University of Texas

78-2518

HC
103
.B85 Business and the
American economy,
1776-2001

78-2518